You Can Observe a Lot by Watching

You Can Observe a Lot by Watching

What I've Learned about Teamwork from the Yankees and Life

YOGI BERRA

with Dave Kaplan

John Wiley & Sons, Inc.

Copyright © 2008 by LTD Enterprises. All rights reserved
Photos copyright © by LTD Enterprises. All rights reserved

Published by John Wiley & Sons, Inc., Hoboken, New Jersey
Published simultaneously in Canada

All photos courtesy of Berra Archives.

For general information about our other products and services, please contact our
Customer Care Department within the United States at (800) 762-2974, outside
the United States at (317) 572-3993 or fax (317) 572-4002.

Wiley also publishes its books in a variety of electronic formats. Some content that
appears in print may not be available in electronic books. For more information
about Wiley products, visit our web site at www.wiley.com.

Library of Congress Cataloging-in-Publication Data:

Berra, Yogi, date.
    You can observe a lot by watching: what I've learned about teamwork
from the Yankees and life / Yogi Berra with Dave Kaplan.
      p. cm.
    Includes index.
    ISBN 978-0-470-07992-8 (cloth)
      1. Berra, Yogi, date. 2. Baseball players—United States—Biography.
    3. Baseball coaches—United States—Biography. 4. Teamwork (Sports)
I. Kaplan, Dave, date. II. Title.
GV865.B46B47 2008
796.357092—dc22
                                                           2008003761

Printed in the United States of America

10 9 8 7 6 5 4 3 2

This book is dedicated to my newest team members, Alexandra and Kay.

—Yogi Berra

To Leah, Emily, and Eva, thank you, thank you very much.

—Dave Kaplan

Contents

Team Player

All I know is we were all
teammates, team-first guys,
because the team good came
before all.

YOU HEAR THE WORDS "team player" all the time, just not in my time. You never heard it on our Yankees teams back when. Never heard of a go-to guy, either. Or someone throwing someone under the bus. Maybe we talked different in the 1950s and '60s, I don't know.

This was before e-mails, cell phones, and this blogging thing. This was before people started comparing sports and business all the time. I don't remember coaches and bosses being control freaks, or managers being micromanagers. When we played there was a bullpen, not a bullpen by committee. To me "at the end of the day" simply meant going to bed. We took risks without having to think outside the box. Now if someone doesn't get with the program or doesn't get on the same page, there's words for that person, too: "Not a team player." I take that to mean a person who doesn't play in the team spirit and is a potential pain in the neck.

Today's sayings are different. People always think I make up my own sayings, but they just come out. I don't know I say them. If you asked me to describe our old Yankees teams, the ones I played on from the late 1940s to the early '60s, what would I say? I'd say we were pretty good. We won an awful lot. In today's business talk we'd be called a high-performance work organization.

All I know is we were all teammates, team-first guys, because the team good came before all. I think it was a behavioral thing, what you learn as a kid. Those skills about getting along on the playground translated into the bigger playing field. Sure, our Yankees teams coordinated well with each other. We all accepted our roles and responsibilities. I always say we were like family. Did we have disagreements and times of trouble? What family doesn't? But we always pulled for each other, trusted each other, counted on each other. That's what all families and teams should do, but don't always.

Before I go on, I have to level. This is no self-help book. I'm no expert on mind games. Dizzy Trout, who used to pitch for the Detroit Tigers, used to tell people, "We pitch to Yogi with psychology because Yogi doesn't know what psychology is." That's true. To me it was hard to think and hit at the same time. Baseball can be a thinking game—90 percent of it is half mental, I said once—but it's still not exactly mental science.

Also, this is no how-to or business book. Baseball is huge business, that's undeniable. Players make small fortunes and teams have luxury taxes. Now there's a moneyball philosophy that values players based on certain statistics that I don't ever suspect about knowing. So I'm no business wizard, either.

What I know pretty good, being in and around sports my whole life, is teamwork. That's being a player on a team who makes a difference, a good difference. You don't need the most great players, just the most team-first, me-last players. Bill Bradley, the former basketball star and senator, said, "The great player is one who makes the worst player on the team good."

If you ask me, the true best players are those who influence their teammates positively. Joe DiMaggio and Mickey Mantle did it with us in our day. They set examples. They gutted through tough times, never made excuses. Everybody trusted and respected them because, to them, being a good teammate was more important than being a star. The Yankees' well-being came before theirs.

Every team has players who may be standouts. I just don't like when standouts try to stand out. In today's culture, it seems like attention-getters become celebrities. In sports you see more hey-look-at-me stuff during a game—players celebrating themselves. Some of these guys who make a tackle on a kickoff go into hysterics, thumping their chests all the way across the field. Why? They did their job. They made a tackle. That's what they're supposed to do.

I know I'm from a different time, and things aren't the same today. Now players are more like entertainers. Still, I wonder if they realize how self-centered and glory-minded they appear. Let me just say I'm not against excitement or exuberance or celebrating a great moment. Don't think we never got real exuberant. People ask if I had planned jumping in Don Larsen's arms during the World Series. All I planned on was giving my best in an important game. Planning

Me, Phil Rizzuto, and Whitey Ford paying tribute to Joe DiMaggio after his death in 1999. He was the best I ever played with.

on catching a perfect game wasn't planned. Sports are emotional. Still, I don't like players who stand and admire their home runs like they finished painting a masterpiece. Or put on a burlesque act after scoring a touchdown. It becomes more about self and showing off than teamwork and working together.

Mostly it doesn't build relationships or loyalty. And what every team and every business needs is loyalty. For me, loyalty to teammates trumped everything. Sure, sports is business, always has been, and there's less loyalty and it's a bigger business than ever. Sometimes I felt management could've been more loyal, at least more generous, during contract time. Actually I had seventeen one-year contracts, probably the most in Yankees history. It was my choice. The front office wanted to give me a two-year or three-year contract, but I felt it was an extra incentive to have the best year I could. I didn't want to get stuck. Of course, I couldn't achieve what I wanted to without the trust and help of my teammates. And vice versa. We just had a loyalty to each other. I know loyalty is more fragile in business. It's fragile in professional sports. People are more transient than ever. But being a trusted coworker or a good teammate should never go out of style.

That's the great thing about watching certain star players in different sports. They get what they give. Guys like Steve Nash and Tim Duncan in basketball, Mariano Rivera and David Ortiz in baseball, and Curtis Martin and Jerome Bettis recently in football; all feel a duty to their teammates. They do what their team needs them to do. They don't embarrass anybody. Teammates love being on their side; they forge a we're-in-it-together atmosphere. When the pressure's on, they raise their game, and that can raise their teammates' play, too.

I used to play a lot of soccer as a kid and still watch it. It's near impossible to rush through the opposing team and be a one-man difference. Just look at David Beckham, and millions do. But I don't look at all the razzmatazz and personal life. The guy's a famous soccer player not because of his looks or goal-scoring, but because of his passing and crossing. A showboater he's not. He makes his teammates better and that matters most to him—"being a team player," he says.

Great players like Beckham will always get heaps of publicity, but what makes them truly great players is how they work within their team. If a teammate needs help, they reach out. Maybe it's a pat on the back or a helpful pointer, or always saying "we" and "us" instead of "me" and "I." Everything to them is team-oriented.

Tom Brady's a lot like that. Being a quarterback who looks like a movie star, he's always the main attraction, but he plays without ego. Bill Belichick, his coach with the Patriots, is a big baseball fan and visited the Yankees at spring training one day. He told me Brady is the first guy at practice and the last to leave. His effect on his teammates is for the good because he's all about the team good. Even in those commercials with his offensive linemen, he's the star simply being a teammate.

LaDainian Tomlinson of the Chargers is another team-first star you don't see enough. Sure he's a heck of an athlete, but he has a humbleness that builds team camaraderie, which you also don't see often. As well as being a record-breaker, he's an attitude-setter with his effort and how much he cares. Right after Tomlinson broke the single-season touchdown record in 2006, he led the group celebration in the end zone. Then he personally thanked every teammate, including the coaches. With Tomlinson, there's never any look-at-me stuff—just respect and appreciation for his teammates.

When your star acts like a regular guy, the regular guys feel as important as the star.

On our Yankees teams, we had regular guys and stars. We didn't have jealousies or finger-pointers. If we had them, I didn't know them. Not everybody was buddy-buddy—you don't need perfect camaraderie to succeed. But we did have team chemistry, even if that word wasn't invented back then. On the Yankees we were all different personalities—some noisy, some not—but we brought out the best in each other. That's a big reason good teams are good teams, and like I said, we must've been pretty good because I played on ten of them that won championships. I also played in fourteen World Series in seventeen seasons, and that's not bad, either.

Here's what I learned in all that time: never prejudge someone, never make excuses and hide from responsibility, and never try not to help a teammate. Like if I saw something that wasn't working, especially with one of our pitchers, I'd try to help fix it in a positive manner. Maybe give a little encouragement, although one of our pitchers, Vic Raschi, wanted no part of my encouraging. Actually Raschi would cuss at me if I came out to talk. So my approach was to get him madder because he pitched better when he was maddest. I'd take a few steps out to the mound and say, "Come on, Onionhead, how many years you've been pitching and you still can't throw a strike? You ought to be ashamed of yourself." Then Raschi would yell at me, "Get back behind your cage where you belong, you sawed-off gorilla." That was real sweet. Then just like that, his fastball would zoom in harder, his control sharper. I guess the lesson is to know what makes your team-mates tick.

You often hear people say, "I'm a team player," but their actions say otherwise. Moping or brooding usually sends a bad message, a self-absorbed message. Mopers and brooders on any team can be a negative drag. Everyone can get in a cranky mood. Every ball-player goes in an occasional slump. Everyone feels rotten once in a while. But bringing a bad case of a bad attitude to work does no good to nobody. That's what Joe DiMaggio used to lay on me. In my second season, I was having trouble mastering being a catcher, so I was being used in right field. It might've affected my mood, because I got bothered at myself for making an out to end an inning and kind of clomped out to my position. DiMaggio, who was always the first guy out to the outfield—kind of like Derek Jeter does in the infield—just looked over at me. The next inning, he came up behind me and said, "Get moving, Yogi, start running." So I started picking it up, with him running alongside me.

"Always run out to your position, Yogi," he said. "It doesn't look good otherwise. Can't get down on yourself. Can't let the other team think they got you down."

Coming from the best player I ever played with, it left an impression. Later I saw DiMaggio go through frustrating stretches, including 1951, his last season, when he really struggled. Yet Joe never sulked. Never made excuses, always looked on the upside. If I'd had a few bad games, I learned not to go around feeling bad. What's sorrier than someone being sorry for himself? When I got home after a loss, my wife, Carmen, would remind me that she was in no mood for my mood, especially since she'd had a tough day herself with the kids. Leave it at the ballpark, she'd say.

If you have a problem, it should be your problem. Don't bring others into it. Once I had a real bad stretch, going 0-for-32, but never admitted I was in a slump—I just said I wasn't hitting.

If you feel bad, going into a shell won't help. DiMaggio was hitting .184 before he began his record fifty-six-game hitting streak. Willie Mays began his career 0-for-21. Jeter even tied me a couple of years ago by going 0-for-32. The good thing about Jeter was he never let it affect him. He was still the first guy to pull for his teammates, first guy on the dugout step. Some guys don't think about anyone else but themselves, but Jeter's head always stayed in the game. When he had that slump, I went over to his locker before a game and told him that Luis Aparicio, who's in the Hall of Fame, once went 0-for-44. I also mentioned that I snapped out of my skid with a home run. He smiled and said, "Thanks, Yog." That night, Jeter snapped out of it with a home run, too.

It seems people compare baseball to life all the time, especially in facing disappointment. Disappointment is just part of life. It comes in every degree. Getting fired from a job is real disappointing. This I know, because I got fired three times as a manager. Being told by Branch Rickey that I'd never become a major-league ballplayer, that wasn't exactly cause for celebration, either. Sure I was disappointed, but disappointments have a bright side. They can make you more determined, tougher. And force you to look at your mistakes or weaknesses.

Facing disappointment is facing life. And it's okay to show emotions. Everyone gets angry and frustrated. Who hasn't flung something in disgust? But being on a team, it's important to keep control of yourself; don't do something you might regret. And you don't have to hide excitement if you've got something to be excited about. Like I said, jumping in Larsen's arms was the emotion of the moment, especially since a perfect game in the World Series had never happened before and hasn't happened since.

Being on a team or in the workplace, think how your emotions affect the people around you. I've been around enough moody, sulking people. Brooding and tantrums aren't going to make anybody around you do or feel any better.

Honestly, I always felt Paul O'Neill reminded me a lot of Mickey Mantle when he'd throw down his helmet or have some other frustration outburst. But all of us always kind of understood the root of Mickey's emotions; he'd be disgusted at himself because he put so much darn pressure on himself. If he failed, he believed he failed his teammates. Same with O'Neill. They were alike not so much because of their outbursts, but because of their passion. They had burning desires to be excellent.

Nobody will ever say Mickey Mantle and Paul O'Neill weren't team-first players. They were. They had a strong influence on their teammates. They worked hard because they wanted to be the best they could. Winning meant more to them than any individual accomplishment. When your top players are focused on team achievements, it can only bring a team together.

Being in New Jersey, I always follow Rutgers even when the football team used to be bad. My son Dale— a real big Rutgers rooter—wouldn't let me write this book without reminding me how they turned the program around in 2006. Not a small reason was that their star runner, Brian Leonard, willingly switched to fullback in his senior year, blocking for tailback Ray Rice for the betterment of the team. Not necessarily for his betterment, since Leonard was a Heisman candidate entering that season. But Leonard got to thinking, "I am scoring and scoring and the team keeps losing and losing. Maybe we'd have a better chance if Rice got most of the carries," and that's exactly what happened. Leonard, who passed up a lot of NFL money to stay at Rutgers for that last season, set a heck of an example of sacrifice. Seeing Rutgers play, you know his selflessness helped their success.

I also watch the New Jersey Devils a lot, and I'm not sure they get enough credit, either. One opposing coach called them "interchangeable parts." I call them one of the most successful teams in sports. Lou Lamoriello's system is the team system. Each player surrenders individual honors for the good of the club—even their more skilled guys and dipsy doodlers. The Devils play great team defense. Their best players all do different things, all do the grunt work, and nobody outworks them.

In every sport, team play always works. Sure you need individual ability. But you also need a readiness to give up your own desires and glory for the sake of the team. It's more true now than ever. Talent is talent, but unless you get everyone pulling together, you're sunk. When some unhappy player wrote "Play for yourself" in the Toronto Blue Jays clubhouse a couple years ago, that was a pretty destructive message if you were his teammate.

Being on a team—any team—is a challenge. Whether you're on the Yankees or a sales team, your goal is always to make yourself the best you can. But it's also to do the little things that can make your teammates or coworkers better, make the team better. You have to emphasize the "we," not the "me," and that means getting your teammates' trust. As a catcher, it took me a bit to earn my pitchers' respect. Mostly because I was a lousy catcher. My first two years I'd throw the ball all over the place, my arm was so scattered. When I put down the sign, our pitchers used their own sign. People asked if the pitchers lost confidence in me. I didn't think so because they never had any.

I improved a lot after Bill Dickey learned me all of his experience, which is how I described it in spring training 1949. It wasn't good English, but it meant what I meant it to mean—Dickey was teaching and I was learning.

Bill Dickey (right), a great man who learned me all his experience. I owe everything to him.

Bill came out of retirement just to help me. He was a heck of a man and was once a heck of a catcher, and he explained that it was my job to quarterback the game. Take the worry out of the pitcher, use your observation to watch the hitters, know their strengths and weaknesses. Learn your pitcher, get a feel for what he does best and not so best. Pitchers think they're smart, but the catcher is there every day and is smarter about the hitters. After my first couple years, I got them to rely on my judgment. They had confidence in me, and I was confident telling them what they should know. I also knew I had to treat each pitcher differ-ent in tough spots. Some I had to nursemaid, some I'd have to whip like Raschi. With a guy like Bob Turley, you'd just have to soothe and sympathize. If he was in trouble, I'd say, "Come on, Bob, you're a good pitcher. These guys just got horseshoes in their pocket. You got good stuff. Now just mow 'em down." With someone like Whitey Ford, you never had to bawl or coax or do anything, really. If he was in a tough spot, I'd just tell him the movie I want to see starts at seven, and it's five now, so let's get this thing over with.

The main thing is to work together, not against each other. I wasn't big on lectures or pep rallies or state secrets at the mound; nobody talked into their gloves back in our day. Usually if I went out to chat, I tried to give the guy a little confidence, get him in tempo. If a guy was pressing, maybe I'd lighten him up. Dickey used to do that. In a tough situation, he'd come out and talk to pitchers about hunting and fishing. One time our relief pitcher Joe Page was struggling, so I went and asked if he had kids. He said no, and I told him he had to have kids because it was the best thing for a family. He began to laugh, then got out of the inning with no trouble.

Now I see pitchers overanalyzing everything. I see them shake signs because they're overthinking or not trusting the catcher. I see unnecessary uncertainty, something you don't need. Look, the pitcher-catcher relationship is the most important in the game. It's almost like a marriage, or like beer and pretzels. It just has to be together, or it won't be. I always wanted my pitcher to believe that everything I did, every little detail or fact I stored in my head, was for the pitcher's own good. Heck, we had the advantage—two guys trying to get one man out. If I knew my business, I figured we were in business and my job was to get the pitcher to do his job. When Allie Reynolds threw two no-hitters in 1951, that's as good as you can do, but he wouldn't take the credit; he told everyone I was the one who did the thinking for him.

That in a nutshell was the kind of team we had. Nobody gloried in individual achievements. It was a shared achievement. Catching Don Larsen's perfect game in the 1956 World Series was my biggest thrill on a ballfield; it was something that's never been done in the history of baseball and never been done since and I was only glad to be part of it.

Reynolds was a great team guy—one of those who quietly did whatever needed to be done. He pitched in pain. One year he had these crackling elbow chips, but he still pitched and won. He took pride in pitching complete games, and completed games for other pitchers. Of course Reynolds also saved me from my worst moment on a ballfield. All he needed was one more out for his second no-hitter, but I lunged and dropped Ted Williams's foul pop-up. I felt awful and wanted to crawl into a hole. Reynolds accidentally stepping on my hand didn't make me feel better, either. But Allie patted me on the back and said don't worry about it. Then as I returned to my position, good ol' Ted started ripping into me, calling me an SOB because now he had to bear down even more. "You had your chance, but you blew it," he said.

So I called the same pitch, same place, and he hit another twisting pop-up, almost in the same place, too. This time I squeezed it, and Reynolds bear-hugged me. It was as if he felt more glad for me than for himself.

When people asked if I liked being a catcher, I'd ask why. Why wouldn't I? It's sometimes a punishment position, but it's the best position because you're the defensive boss. You see the whole field and know where each of the seven fielders should be. You call the pitches and direct where they should go. You advise when advice is needed. You set the pace. It's like Miller Huggins, the manager on those old Yankees teams with Ruth and Gehrig, said: "A good catcher is the quarterback, the carburetor, the lead dog, the pulse taker, the traffic cop, and sometimes a lot of unprintable things, but no team gets very far without one."

A good catcher also does all the little things, which sometimes become the real important things. Me, personally, I always figured there were a bunch of different ways to help my team, regardless if I went 0-for-4 at the plate. I knew the team needed me to call a good game, keep our pitcher in a groove, block bad pitches, throw runners out, and pop out of a squat and sprint to back up first on infield plays.

Catching's a great position and I got no regrets. But it's tough, too, don't get me wrong. Johnny Bench and any good catcher will tell you it can be pretty grueling. Johnny had it a little worse than me before he started playing another position. As a catcher, he had four broken bones in his feet, constant back pain, circulation problem in his hands, shoulder surgery, and gnarled toenails. *Sports Illustrated* figured he also did over 330,000 deep knee bends, one for each pitch. I was luckier. I was short and didn't have that far to squat. My worst injury was a foul tip by Bobby Avila of Cleveland in 1957 that cracked my double-bar mask and broke my nose.

If you want to be a catcher, you better want it. And you better work at it. You also better have an inner conceit, a confidence that you can meet any situation. If you see something wrong, do something. Me and Whitey Ford always had a perfect rapport, but one time in a World Series he threw a slider, which he never used to throw. After the batter got a hit, I walked to the mound and told him, "No more." And Whitey, who only was the winningest pitcher in Yankee history, gave me that smart-aleck smile and said, "Come on, Yog, I'm experimenting." I told him to experiment in the off-season, not the World Series, and that was that.

To me, one of the best parts about catching was being in the game. It's the most sociable position on the ballclub. I mean, you're there every pitch, you get to talk to the hitters, which I enjoyed because you find out what they're like. I didn't talk to the new ones until I got to know them. Never did I distract a hitter by talking during the pitch—that's bad sportsmanship. But I'd make a little conversation, a little ribbing, and it was fun. That's how I became pals with Larry Doby and Ted Williams, asking about their family, where they were eating after the game, or recommending a movie I'd just seen. I'd ask Ted about fishing, which he loved as much as hitting. Yet Ted had his limits, and if I affected his concentration too much, he'd let me know. "Okay, shut up, you little dago," he'd say.

Maybe I talked a lot behind the plate, but I didn't compare to my pal Joe Garagiola. Joe made so many guys laugh, they had to step out of the batter's box. But he'll tell you at least once his gabbing blew up in his face. During a tight game in St. Louis, Joe tried to keep Stan Musial, his old Cardinals teammate, from concentrating on the pitch. "Hey, Stan," he said, "about ten of us fellows are coming over to your restaurant with our wives for dinner. Do we need to make a reservation?"

Stan didn't answer, just kept his eyes squared on the pitch, which was a strike.

"Should we take taxis, or do you have enough parking space near the restaurant?" Joe asked just before the next pitch. Stan still didn't answer and was starting to get a little annoyed.

Joe was sure now he'd really gotten Musial off stride. He called for the next pitch, which Musial smacked for a home run into the right-field bleachers at Sportsman's Park. After he rounded the bases, he turned to Garagiola as he crossed home and said, "How do you people like your steaks?"

To me, the best part of being a catcher was being able to help the team in different ways. Most important was calling a good game, which I think I did good because I studied the hitters an awful lot. There were no computers or statistical stuff like today, so I just did old-fashioned observing. As I've said, you could observe a lot by watching, so I observed and watched and learned. Casey Stengel used to say I knew every hitter in the league except myself. That's because I never met a pitch I wouldn't swing at. My philosophy, if you want to call it that, was if I could see it, I could hit it. No question, I liked being a catcher. But I *loved* being a hitter.

Good team guys somehow find a way to do what's best for their team. Good team guys come through when it matters most. I've been on both sides, believe me. The Yankees probably suffered their toughest losses to swallow—the 1955 World Series and 2004 American League Championship Series (ALCS)—because of great efforts by great team players.

To this day, and it's been over a darn half century already, people always remind me of Jackie Robinson stealing home in game 1 of the 1955 World Series. Say "Jackie Robinson," I say "Out." He was called safe, but he was really out, and I'll never admit otherwise. But I've gotten calmer about it over the years, appreciating what Jackie did—even if he was out—for the benefit of his team. At that time, Jackie's legs were aching and brittle, he was thirty-six years old and not his old self. And at that time, we were winning 6–4 in the eighth inning, so Jackie's run didn't mean anything, or so everyone thought.

Nobody knew better than me what kind of competitor Jackie was—I played against him in the International League in 1946 when he was with Montreal and I was at Newark. He did everything to eliminate us in the playoffs that year. As Leo Durocher used to say, Jackie Robinson could beat you in more ways than anybody he ever saw.

And in my rookie year with the Yankees in 1947, Jackie stole three bases off us—I blame me—in the World Series. When reporters asked me before the Series about him, I said I wasn't worried. I might've been trying to psych myself up because I hadn't been catching long. But Jackie helped upset my psyche. He just had a knack for unsettling a pitcher and a catcher and the entire defense with his baserunning.

Stealing home is the most daring, risky act in baseball, and something you never see anymore. Jackie did it some nineteen times.

Even though we had a two-run lead in the eighth inning in game 1 of the '55 World Series, Whitey Ford said he was kind of expecting Jackie to steal home. In fact, he dared him to do it by taking a long windup but still got me the ball in plenty of time. He got it right where it had to be, and Jackie slid right into the tag. No question about it, except Bill Summers was a short umpire and I don't think he saw it too good. Naturally I got aggressively upset and ranted at Summers for a good while. Maybe he knew he blew it, because he didn't eject me. And Frank Kellert, the Brooklyn batter during the play, also acknowledged later that Jackie was out. Actually he didn't say it until he got traded by the Dodgers a few days after the World Series, but Kellert had the best view of anyone.

Jackie's steal didn't change the game. The Dodgers still lost, 6–5. Afterward, I was still burned and thought it wasn't a smart baseball play and said so. So did a lot of people, even accusing Jackie of showboating. But I learned later that he wasn't—he was just trying to ignite a spark. He feared his team was psychologically affected by the Yankees (we'd beaten them in our previous five World Series). And that was his way—stealing home on his own, no orders—to rouse his teammates. Remember, Jackie wasn't the same player in 1955; there was lots of talk that year that he was over the hill, that the Dodgers were going to get rid of him. But as he said before the season, "If I find out I can't do justice to myself and give the ballclub its due, I'll retire."

That season he platooned at third with Don Hoak and missed game 7 of the World Series because of an Achilles' strain. But he was still the ingredient that got the Dodgers boiling, and they finally beat us in '55 for the only time.

After Johnny Podres blanked us in game 7, I went into the visiting clubhouse where the Dodgers were celebrating like mad. I congratulated Podres and saw Pee Wee Reese and Jackie by their lockers. They were happy but looked drained. I think they knew their careers were almost over. But I knew how much beating us meant to them and congratulated them, too.

A year later, we returned the favor and beat the Dodgers in seven. Right after that '56 Series, Jackie came into our clubhouse and put his arm around me. He never played another game in baseball.

You won't hear me denying we had a fierce rivalry with the Dodgers. But we had great respect for those guys. We were friends. We barnstormed in the off-season together. They were largely a great team because Pee Wee and Jackie were great team guys. Of course Pee Wee welcomed Jackie as he would any other ballplayer when he joined the team. He made it plain that if anyone said anything or did anything out of line, just because Jackie was black, he'd always defend Jackie's right to play for the Dodgers—if he was good enough.

As a teammate, you always want to count on your teammates. To me, that kind of sums up why the Red Sox made that comeback to win the ALCS against the Yankees in 2004. Sure, the Yankees should've won—heck, they were up 3–0 in games and three outs away from winning. The Red Sox were exhausted and reeling. Were the Yankees too confident? Maybe. But Boston's pitchers really made it happen. They sacrificed for their teammates, doing whatever was needed to get back in the Series. When the Red Sox were getting pummeled in game 3, they practically had no pitchers left. So Tim Wakefield, who was supposed to start game 4, walked up to manager Terry Francona and volunteered to help. That meant sacrificing his start and mopping up in a 19–8 blowout.

Don't think that unselfishness went unnoticed. Boston's other tired pitchers mustered enough to get them back in the Series. Francona knew it all started with Wakefield. He kept saying he was proud to manage a player with that attitude. That Red Sox team all had that attitude. Their cliques were just one clique; everybody got along and pulled together. It did remind me of our teams in the early '50s. If needed, Allie Reynolds would come in relief the day after he started. Some people told him he was crazy, warning him that he'd shorten his career. But Allie's feeling was that if he could help, he would.

In those 2004 playoffs, the Red Sox had the right karma, the Yankees didn't. Especially in game 7, when the Yankees had to use a veteran pitcher, Kevin Brown, who never really endeared himself to anyone. He'd hurt himself punching a wall earlier that season. When he got knocked out of the game early, he disappeared, like he wasn't part of the team.

I'll always be a Yankee fan, but I couldn't help but respect the Red Sox, who I never thought would ever beat us. I appreciated how Terry Francona (whose dad, Tito, I played against and always liked) never panicked and did a heck of a job.

And you had to appreciate Wakefield after his ordeal in 2003. Giving up a crushing homer like he did to Aaron Boone in the ALCS could've destroyed a lot of guys. But it didn't destroy Wakefield, and nobody respected that more than Joe Torre. After losing to the Red Sox, Joe congratulated Francona, then called Wakefield to tell him he wasn't happy he beat us but was glad for him getting to the World Series.

Over the last eight years, I've spent a lot of time in Joe's office when I go to Yankee Stadium. We've known each other a long time, and there's hardly anybody I respect more. Joe just does things the right way. He respects the game. He handles problems and pressure better than anyone I know. Calm, loyal, trusting, honest, he's everything you want in a manager. Plus he never loses perspective, and that's not easy in New York. People wanted him fired since he hadn't won a World Series since 2000. They forget the Yankees hadn't won since '78—until Joe got there.

That's when Joe brought a team-first attitude. He didn't tolerate moodiness or selfishness. Guys bought into the fundamentals, doing the little things, supporting each other. The Yankees of the late '90s didn't necessarily have the biggest stars; they had the best working-together guys. That's what Joe emphasized, and that's why they won four world championships in five years.

One thing that really distinguishes the Yankees is how they honor the past—old past and new past. They're the only team that celebrates Old-Timers' Day. When guys like David Cone and Darryl Strawberry, who are both half my age, show up as Old-Timers, I'm wondering what that makes me.

I know Scott Brosius at first wasn't crazy about coming to the 2007 event. But I know he'll never regret or forget it, either. He got maybe the loudest ovation from the fans, louder than for Whitey or Reggie or any of the great Yankee stars. He couldn't believe it, either.

To me, that was the fans' way of saying thanks. Thanks for being a great team guy who helped the Yankees win championships. All this for a third baseman who nobody in baseball wanted after the 1997 season—there's not a big market for .203 hitters. But the Yankees saw something in Brosius, who played seven years in Oakland. They saw he was a hard worker. If he wasn't hitting, at least his defense never went in a slump. With the Yankees he was a bottom-of-the-order guy. But he never played better and became the MVP of the 1998 World Series. Why? I think the team's pride and teamwork got contagious. Brosius fit right in with a bunch of guys who did all the little things correctly.

People often asked me to compare those Yankees teams with our Yankees teams in the '50s and '60s.

The major similarity was the guys pulling together—individual goals never mattered. Paul Molitor, a Hall of Famer who was winding up his twenty-year career in 1998, said the Yankees that season may have been the best team he'd ever seen. "On top of pitching, defense, and the ability to run the bases, they have a very professional group of people," he said. "The thing that I think sets them apart is that they have great clutch hitters who are patient enough to wait for their pitch. If they walk, fine. The next guy can get it done. There's never a sense of urgency to be *the* guy." Brosius was basically a guy who was one of the guys. He was one of a bunch that included Paul O'Neill, Tino Martinez, and Luis Sojo. And the bigger or tighter the game, the tougher they were.

On our teams everyone's ego took a backseat to the team ego. That's what a lot of businesses emphasize today, people who are able to work in teams. Teamwork in sports is a lot like the working world. All teams are made up of individuals, all with different skills and experience. But unless you instill a team attitude, you'll lose the teamness in the team. It goes for all teams, whether it's a peewee hockey team or a business management team. You need unselfishness. You need to think positive and work together; our Yankees teams were positively close-knit. Not to sound like that psychology guy Dr. Phil, but if you don't have a good attitude in anything you do, nothing you do will be that good.

We were good because we motivated each other and never wanted to let anyone down. That's why nobody on our teams tolerated mental mistakes, which are the worst mistakes you can make. Errors everyone makes.

People are human. But bonehead mistakes—the mental ones—that's another thing. They're almost unforgivable because it means your head isn't 100 percent in the game. They're self-centered mistakes. In the late '90s the Yankees had a second baseman, Chuck Knoblauch, who made a terrible lapse—he argued with an umpire while the ball was rolling away and still in play. Worse, it came in the playoffs. More worse, it cost the Yankees a game. It was such a bad mental breakdown that Knoblauch apologized to his teammates.

I don't remember anyone apologizing to anyone on our teams. But if you messed up mentally—missed a sign, threw to the wrong base, or forgot the situation—you'd get a certain glare from Joe DiMaggio. Or a severe warning from Hank Bauer. And you didn't dare ever do it again.

It can happen to the best, though. Not too many players I know played harder or were better team leaders than Frank Robinson. One time, though, he didn't run all out on a long hit, thinking it was going over the fence, and got thrown out at second. After the game he left a hundred-dollar bill on his manager's desk with a note: "I embarrassed you. I embarrassed the team. I embarrassed baseball and most of all I embarrassed myself."

Everyone does something embarrassing at some point; people happen to be human. I had some moments I'd like to forget. Who wouldn't? In the 1947 World Series, my rookie season, the Dodgers ran ragged on me. The writer Red Smith said they stole everything but my chest protector, and Connie Mack said he'd never seen worse catching in his life. That we won the Series helped ease the sting, but I never forgot that brutal feeling.

One thing, it awakened my pride. Striking out at the plate was also a terrible feeling. To me that was personal failure, an embarrassment. To this day, I don't like when guys strike out, because it's an unproductive out that in no way helps the team. When people ask me what I'm individually proud of, I don't like to boast. But I tell them to look at my record in 1950. For the record, I had twelve strikeouts in 597 at-bats. People always ask when an athlete should quit. To me that's easy. When you can't help your team anymore. When I joined the Mets in 1965 as a coach, I'd been retired as a player. But they asked me to play a few games. When I struck out three times in one game against Tony Cloninger—I used to go a month without three strikeouts—that was it and I knew it.

I managed Willie Mays on the Mets in 1973, although he wasn't Willie Mays anymore. He was forty-one and couldn't do what he used to, so it was a tough situation. Baseball was his life. He wanted to go out on a high note in New York, where he'd started his career. He was good to our younger guys, real professional, but he had a couple of embarrassing moments on the field. That wasn't the Willie anyone wanted to remember, so he quit, a couple of seasons later than he should've.

Mickey Mantle once told me he wished he'd retired after the '64 season, when I managed him also. Although Mickey was semicrippled that year, he still hit thirty-five homers and drove in over a hundred runs. He liked to remind me I sucked out the last good season from him. His good days were over. In those last gimpy years, though, he remained a good team guy, helping out Bobby Murcer, who was hyped as the "next Mantle"—both were Okies and originally shortstops who were rushed through the minors. But Mickey kept reminding Bobby to be himself, forget the comparisons. And he did by having a good career himself.

Before the '69 season, Mickey knew that he had overstayed, so he retired. When he said he never wanted to embarrass himself on the field, or hurt the team, that's what he believed. He always gave his most and more.

Knowing exactly when to quit is one thing. But if you always try as hard as you can, there's nothing to be sorry for. Saying something dumb after a loss, you may be sorry. Hurting your team by getting injured, of course you're sorry. But there's no need to apologize, unless you do something dumb-headed like bust up your hand by punching a wall.

When Hideki Matsui of the Yankees broke his wrist diving for a ball during the 2006 season, I think he felt worse for his teammates than for himself. He apologized to them. I know Joe Torre and the team were touched by his sincerity and Japanese attitude, where the team always comes above the individual. In Japan, where Matsui was a star, they always practice long and hard, maybe too much. The idea is toughening the player to prevent injuries. Well, that I don't know. As I said, my worst injury was getting my nose broken, but it was also my best injury since it really cleared my sinuses.

My Bad

Being on a team means taking responsibility and protecting teammates. . . . Being accountable, protecting a teammate, is something people always remember.

NOWADAYS YOU HEAR PEOPLE apologize without apologizing. They say, "My bad," meaning it's my fault, I messed that up. But it doesn't really mean he or she is sorry.

Much worse is blaming a teammate for something you screwed up yourself—that's worse than bad. That's how you lose everyone's respect. I've heard players blame the media or the weather or a pregame meal, any excuse they can find. But you can't hide behind the team by blaming a teammate. It doesn't work. Blaming someone else for taking a substance you put in your body? Also worse than bad.

Being on a team means taking responsibility and protecting teammates. I never heard a guy on our team ever say after a loss or a bad play, "Hey, not my fault." You never, ever want to have a teammate not believe in you. Reporters made a big deal during game 3 of the 1952 World Series when our pitcher Tom Gorman, who had a tricky sinker, threw a pitch past me. Two runs scored, and we lost the game, 5–3. The writers believed that since he was a rookie in his first World Series, he'd misunderstood my signals. When I heard this, I called them over. "Gorman didn't do nothing wrong," I told them. "He didn't cross me up, and don't none of you guys believe him if he says he did. I messed up the play. Blame me, not him."

I know that meant a lot to Tom, because he told me so. The next spring he said my support was the "most generous thing anyone ever did for me . . . Yogi was trying to protect a young kid like me from being branded a goat, as unselfish an act as I've ever experienced. I crossed him up. The blame was mine, not Yogi's."

I'm not ready for sainthood. It's just the right team thing to take responsibility and not fault anybody or anything—somebody's got to win, somebody's got to lose, because life is like that. You're not supposed to win every game. That's what I always tell kids at our museum. Everyone hurts when they lose. It's disappointing. When you're used to winning, it's hard to accept being second best. On our teams, we hated to lose. What competitor doesn't? But I think we all had a handle on it.

We won 103 games in 1954 but still finished in second place to the Indians. They were just better, what can you say?

When the Dodgers finally beat us in the 1955 World Series, nobody was thrilled. But nobody kicked any chairs across the dressing room. Nobody punished themselves. They were tough games. But somebody had to lose, and it was us. Whenever we did lose, Casey Stengel especially was gracious. Never made excuses, always congratulated the other guy for playing better.

I think that's important for any player on any team. If you lose, deal with it. It's what you learn from the experience that matters. Learn what you could do differently next time. If you did all that it was humanly possible to do, take the good in that. A good competitor is always modest in victory, gracious in defeat.

When the Yankees lost that heartbreaking 2001 World Series to Arizona, they handled it the right way. Derek Jeter probably spoke for everyone when he said, "We didn't give them anything. They earned it. Up 2–1, bottom of the ninth, Mariano [Rivera] on the mound. . . . They deserve to be champions."

Sometimes losing brings out the best in people, even politicians. So many of them go around saying terrible things. They act brutal so they can win. Then when they lose, they act respectful and say the right things. It's like they're better at losing than winning. They stop blaming everybody and everything.

Still, this is a blame culture. In youth sports especially. You hear parents and kids complain about umpires or teammates all the time. That stinks because it gives kids excuses. Teaches them it's always someone else's fault. When a nine-year-old kid says, "We lost because the refs blew it," that should tell you something. It tells you the kid probably echoed what he heard from an adult. Kids are sponges, they absorb.

Blaming something or somebody happens all the time. It's sour-graping. It's the easy out. Too many professional people blame everything and everybody but themselves. You sure don't inspire trust that way. All the blaming by politicians and government agencies after Hurricane Katrina—all of it solved nothing. The levees broke, people weren't evacuated, and New Orleans was a mess. All the blamers sounded like a kid who lost his homework.

When you blame, you kind of lose perspective. It's like a fat lady blaming a fast-food place for her being fat. It's weaseling out of responsibility. ESPN even developed this program that gave reasons why you shouldn't blame someone who's gotten blamed. Still, there's something about sports—at every level— that gets too many people in a blame trap. I think it's mostly frustration and emotion. People protect themselves from blame by blaming. You think the Chicago Cubs lost the National League championship in 2003 because a fan interfered with a foul ball when the Cubs had a 3–0 lead? Thousands of Cubs fans (and some of the players) sure think so.

Losing fuels a lot of blame. I'm not suggesting some don't deserve blame for losing. But team players have a responsibility not to point fingers. It helps nobody, solves nothing. It even makes things worse. I'm a Giants football fan and always liked Tiki Barber. He played the game right, shared the credit for his success. But after the Giants lost to Carolina in the 2006 playoffs, he caught heck by saying the Giants were "outcoached." The media made a big deal of it, saying he was blaming his own coach, Tom Coughlin. I don't think that's what Tiki intended. He was being honest, maybe too honest, and was frustrated. Later he met with Coughlin, then clarified his comments to the media. He owned up to his blameworthy mistake.

The best team players are stand-up, no-excuses players. Those players always have the respect of their teammates. Mickey Mantle was that guy for us with the Yankees.

Nobody cared that he was making $100,000 in the early '60s, which was a lot of money back then (and almost twice what me and Whitey Ford were making). How could anyone resent him? There wasn't anything Mickey wouldn't do to help the team. His knees were shot, but he never complained or made excuses. He always played as hard as he could and was harder on himself than any player I ever saw. When he'd limp into the clubhouse before a game, Casey would say, "Oh, I see you can't play today." And Mickey would follow him right into his office demanding to be put in the lineup.

Mickey never blamed anybody or anything. Always was respectful of his teammates and his manager, who was always tough on him. Always had his teammates' backs, even during the most crushing disappointment of his career, losing the 1960 World Series. No way we should've lost—we outscored the Pirates 55–27. But we lost a couple of close ones, including game 7, when Bill Mazeroski hit a homer over my head in left field in the ninth inning. There could've been a lot of blame to go around, too. Casey made some questionable moves, like not starting Whitey Ford in game 1 and using Ralph Terry in relief to pitch to Mazeroski. Tony Kubek got the bad hop, Jim Coates forgot to cover first in the eighth inning on Roberto Clemente's grounder, and Terry threw a bad pitch. It was all tough to swallow. Mickey sat in the trainer's room, crying,

You can't always win, because somebody's got to lose.
I'm headed for the showers, followed by Tony Kubek, Marv
Throneberry (briefly a Yankee), and Johnny Kucks in 1959.

feeling worse than he ever did after a loss. But neither he nor anybody else blamed anybody. When a reporter asked me if there was one reason we lost the Series, I just said, "We made too many wrong mistakes." Didn't say who, just we.

If you're a good teammate, be responsible for what you say. Even if you're feeling awful, wronged, frustrated, or worse. Take a pause. Don't say something you'll regret. The last thing you want to do is lose your teammates. That's what the U.S. women's goalie did in the 2007 World Cup semifinals. The goalie, Hope Solo, was upset at her coach for benching her—that you can understand. Everyone has a right to think they deserve to play. And she had every right to express her frustration. It's a free country. But I don't think she realized the damage she caused within her team with her words. When she said she would've made those saves in her team's 4–0 loss, she sounded egotistical. Worse, she belittled the other goalie, her teammate, in public. Maybe not intentionally. But teammates are supposed to support teammates—and she clearly didn't. She didn't mean to, but she made it sound like her teammates weren't good enough without her. You can't blame her teammates for wanting her off the team, and that's what happened.

Whatever trouble you're in, don't pawn it off on a teammate. Don't blame, don't insinuate blame. One of the most sacred team rules is the Las Vegas rule—whatever happens in the clubhouse stays in the clubhouse. It's a code of honor. It's hard to fully trust or count on every teammate, not everyone's the same. But a true teammate never rats out another. A good teammate is loyal to both himself and his teammates.

One of my favorite baseball movies is *Eight Men Out,* the story about the White Sox players who took payoffs to throw the 1919 World Series. No excusing what those players did, no matter the circumstances. To me it was a case of guys willing to do something wrong because they saw enough others doing it. That's why you had to sympathize a bit for a guy like Buck Weaver, who didn't take part in the fix. Yet he didn't inform anyone about it, either. He just played hard the whole Series, never betraying himself or his team. The sad thing is he got banished from baseball forever, too.

Scandals happen. Players are people. They cheat, they take shortcuts, they want an edge. It's no secret that's why baseball has this steroids mess. Truthfully, I get tired of being asked about steroids, so I don't answer. What can you say? I'll just say a good teammate doesn't rat out another teammate—he keeps matters in-house.

Fortunately, I never saw a teammate doing harmful stuff to himself. If I did, I wouldn't blab it to the world. If a teammate's in trouble, any kind of trouble, you try to help. The team's a family.

You wonder about players who aren't accountable for their trouble. You wonder if they understand trust or what being on a team really means.

In all my years with the Yankees, it's hard to think of anyone betraying teammates. Well, there was Jim Bouton. Although he wrote *Ball Four* after he'd left the Yankees, guys didn't like what he wrote. To me Bouton was a good teammate, and he pitched great ball for me when I managed the club in 1964. What he wrote was supposedly for entertainment. But telling embarrassing stuff about Mickey Mantle and other former teammates felt like a betrayal. It took years and years for guys to forgive him.

I'd always been brought up believing that teammates protect teammates. They're there for them, always. And good teammates make no excuses, period. I'd always heard how Mickey Owen did exactly that after his famous passed ball in game 4 of the 1941 World Series helped the Yankees beat the Brooklyn Dodgers. It was one of the all-time heartbreakers, and that's what Owen's most known for. Yet Phil Rizzuto and Tommy Henrich always said Owen wasn't to blame—they insist that pitcher Hugh Casey's breaking ball was definitely a spitball. But after the game Owen said he'd called for a low inside curve, Henrich's weakness, and he should've shifted his feet a few inches to make sure. "It was one of the greatest curves Casey or any other pitcher ever threw," he said. "The fault was mine. I'm not sorry for myself. I'm sorry for what I've done to the other fellows." The next day, Rizzuto said Owen got the biggest ovation he ever heard in Ebbets Field.

Successful teams are based on trust and loyalty. Once you betray that trust and loyalty, you got issues. Of all people, Peyton Manning once did just that. It almost didn't matter that he was the hardest-working or most dedicated player in the NFL. Or was the team leader who always gave team-first responses in interviews. What mattered were his words after the Colts lost to Pittsburgh in the 2006 AFC Championship Game. "I'm trying to be a good teammate here. Let's just say we had some problems with protection." The way it was repeated over and over, you'd think he'd just declared war on a country.

He did say the obvious. The Colts couldn't handle the blitz. But maybe he should've just praised the Steelers defense. Instead Manning got pounded for not taking responsibility, for quasi-blaming his teammates. He didn't mean it that way, but that's how it came out.

The good thing is his teammates never gave up on him, and he learned a lesson. "Ever since I said that, I've really been probably more careful than I've ever been before," he said. "I have a hard time even seeing how it could have been interpreted that way, and it still bothers me that it was. But since it happened, my approach has been, 'Do less, say less, go play.'"

Good approach. He helped the Colts win the Super Bowl the next year. Then he restructured his contract to give the team more salary cap room. Did he become a team player overnight? No, he just became more aware of the power of words.

Did anyone ever hear Derek Jeter criticize a team-mate? Me neither. But I'm amazed when people say he could be a better team guy. If I had a criticism of Jeter, it's his signature, which is a little loopy. When I visit Yankee Stadium, I kid around with him in the locker room and get on him a bit if he struck out on a bad ball. When he tells me I used to swing at them, I remind him I hit those, he doesn't. That's about it. He's a good kid, a good leader. When he talks to the media, he never says anything except "we." You won't find a ballplayer who doesn't admire or respect the way he goes about his business. Just because he and Alex

Rodriguez aren't the best of chums, it doesn't mean Jeter doesn't cheer or support him. Just because they don't go out to dinner, it doesn't mean he doesn't want to see A-Rod at his best. Sometimes that camaraderie thing is overrated. Don't tell me everyone loves each of their coworkers.

Here's the thing about Jeter. He's all about the team. Being a Yankee is special to him, and it comes with responsibility. He's a good leader because he always knows and does what's right. He reminds me a lot of DiMaggio that way. There was a game in 1998 when a bloop fell in between Jeter and the centerfielder and the leftfielder. David Wells was pitching and he wasn't happy. He shot this glare at the guys, steamed that they let him down. So Jeter called time and came to the mound. "We don't do that stuff here," he told Wells. "That's not right and you know it. We're all out here trying. That's baloney."

That's one of the truest things every teammate should know. Never embarrass another teammate. It's a hurtful thing to do and can't do any good. Criticizing a teammate like that isn't a teammate's job.

I'll always remember the 1950 World Series against the Phillies, when Whitey Ford was one out away from a complete game shutout in game 4. But Gene Woodling lost a ball in the sun in left field, and two runners scored. Whitey was a real cocky rookie then. He wanted badly to finish the game. But he got taken out right then by Casey Stengel, who was pretty ticked at Woodling. Whitey could've been upset, too. But he knew the last thing his teammate was trying to do was muff a play. Allie Reynolds came in, got the last out, and we were

Me and Whitey Ford at the 1999 World Series, where he pitched the ceremonial ball to me. Whitey still leads all Yankee pitchers in games, innings, wins, strikeouts, and shutouts, and he pitched $33\frac{2}{3}$ consecutive scoreless innings in the World Series. That's not bad.

champions. In the clubhouse afterward, Whitey gave Gene a hug, and that was that.

In all the years I played with him, I never saw Whitey ever knock a teammate. He was the opposite. He was aware of everyone's feelings. At the end of the 1956 season, Whitey was going for his twentieth win—it was a big deal since he'd never won twenty before. But we lost 1–0, and the only run scored when Mickey Mantle dropped a ball in centerfield. After the game Mickey was a mess. He was near tears. He didn't have the heart to face Whitey, knowing that he was responsible for the loss. So Whitey goes to Mickey's locker, puts his hand on his shoulder, and says, "Forget it, kid. Let's have a beer."

That's how Whitey was. He'd also always go out of his way to talk to a younger player. He wanted everyone to feel part of the Yankees. Whitey was a fun guy, liked to stay out late. Mickey always said Whitey took five years off his life, but he never would've had so much fun. When it came to pitching and winning big games, though, he never fooled around. He was smart, cool, and so crafty he could throw three different curveballs.

Mostly he liked keeping everyone loose, being one of the guys. When he wasn't pitching, he dug up holes for his own golf course under the right-field bleachers in Yankee Stadium. He and Bill Stafford, one of our young pitchers, would have putting contests using bats and baseballs.

Whitey's one of those guys who was always loyal to his teammates. That's all we knew on the Yankees. All my old teammates—guys like Moose Skowron, Bobby Richardson, Bob Turley—are the most loyal people

I know. It's been almost fifty years since we were teammates. But if they ask me for a favor tomorrow, I do it. When I ask them to come to our museum charity golf event in New Jersey, they come from wherever they are to be here. I can't thank them enough and get a little misty-eyed whenever I see them. They'll always be my teammates. They always remind me of what we accomplished together.

In a way we were like brothers, and Hank Bauer was really a big brother to Mickey and Moose. Heck, he gave Mickey his first beer. Mostly he helped younger guys a lot when they were coming up. Hank was one of those guys everybody liked because you had to love him. All those guys on the Yankees resembled that.

A few years ago, Whitey had some kind of health issue and I heard people were having trouble reaching him. So I called him and asked, "Whitey, you dead yet?" He understood what I meant and told me he appreciated it. Moose had a double bypass in 1995, the same time Mickey was going through his liver transplant. But Mickey was so concerned about Moose that he called him every day. Even when Moose got home from the hospital, Mickey called to see if he was okay. When Moose said yes, Mickey told him, "Great, the only reason I ask is that most people who have that operation only live two days."

Mickey always made you laugh. He always had a caring attitude, one reason we all appreciated him. And he was team-first all the way—nothing he wouldn't do to help a teammate. The way he played, real hurt and all, was because he cared. He cared about whatever it took to help the team. I always said there's no telling how good he'd be if he had two good legs. But even with those damaged knees, he was a great baserunner and centerfielder and did so many things real grand. Baseball's gone crazy with statistics, but one good stat to me is always runs scored. From 1953 to 1961, Mickey scored a hundred or more runs a season. Another good one is twenty-four hundred games, roughly how many Mickey played.

Guys always felt that extra confidence with Mickey playing. They knew they had a better chance of winning. I don't know if Mickey ever called himself a leader or a team player. Most important to him was being a great teammate, which he was.

The Essence of a Teammate

My definition of another great team guy is Don Baylor. . . . His focus was playing the game right, being a positive influence. When clubs needed to "rent a leader," they acquired Baylor and got the best leadership and aggressiveness anywhere.

MY DEFINITION OF ANOTHER great team guy is Don Baylor. How many guys play on three different World Series teams in three straight years? I don't know, but Baylor did. His focus was playing the game right, being a positive influence. When clubs needed to "rent a leader," they acquired Baylor and got the best leadership and aggressiveness anywhere.

I got to manage him with the Yankees in 1984 and felt lucky to have him. Nobody helped his teammates more or got more respect. I remember in our spring training opener, Baylor chewed out a guy for failing to run out a grounder. When he spoke, everyone listened. He was like a big brother to Don Mattingly, who was just a kid, and he was always helping Dave Winfield, a veteran who was taking a lot of grief from George Steinbrenner. And both had great seasons—Mattingly won the batting title at .343 and Winfield was right behind.

When the Tigers started off 35–5 that year, it obviously wasn't going to be our year. But I wanted to keep our team playing hard and together all season. So I asked Baylor, a guy everyone respected, to help keep the guys on their toes. I asked him to run a kangaroo court, a good way to keep things light by fining guys for missing signs or wearing ugly clothes. It's also a good way to keep guys' minds on executing. As judge, Baylor gave out fines for any screwup.

Say if a pitcher allowed a hit on an 0–2 count, it'd cost him five bucks. If a batter didn't move the runners up with less than two outs, it'd cost him, too. Baylor made it fun. Back then we had Phil Niekro, who was forty-five, just released from the Braves, and wanted to show he wasn't done. But one day Knucksie gave up a grand slam on an 0–2 pitch. So Baylor fined him $100, figuring on $25 for each run. I don't know if that made an impact on Knucksie, but I know he won sixteen games for us that season and made the All-Star team.

The saying is that getting hit by a pitch is "taking one for the team." Aside from Craig Biggio, nobody took more for his team than Baylor. Throughout his career, he crowded the plate to take away the pitcher's confidence of throwing inside. So he got plunked an awful lot; he still has the Yankee record by getting hit twenty-four times in one season. Minnie Minoso would do the same for the White Sox in the 1950s. Always gladly take a beaning to get on first base.

In my book, though, there's never been a guy who's meant more to one team for so long than Johnny Pesky. We had a great rivalry with the Red Sox in the late 1940s and '50s, and the 1949 pennant race was one

Phil Rizzuto was my teammate for life—there's
nothing we wouldn't do for each other.

of the toughest. Those guys could play—Ted Williams, Dom DiMaggio, Bobby Doerr, and Pesky, who gave everything to that club and still does. Back then, he was one of the top shortstops, a great hit-and-run guy, did everything right. Even after he retired he pitched batting practice, became a scout, manager, broadcaster— he told me he'd probably die in a Boston uniform. Everything to Johnny was team, team, team, and he had a great loyalty to Ted Williams, whom he jokingly called God. When World War II broke out, I think Ted made him find religion by talking him into going into the flight program with him.

When I managed my first game as a Yankee in 1964, it felt only right that Johnny Pesky was there as Red Sox manager. We kidded with each other before the game; there was a rainout the day before, and his rookie star, Tony Conigliaro, overslept and missed the bus to Yankee Stadium. Johnny fined him $10, so I told Johnny that he was already a ruthless manager. Actually Conigliaro was only a teenager but furious at himself for being so irresponsible. He was telling everyone he should've been fined $1,000 and suspended. But Johnny had a fatherly talk with him, warned him that he was in the big leagues now, and Conigliaro went on to have a great season. Of course, Johnny got fired that year, and so did I. Supposedly we both didn't control our players. That I don't know. I do know the Red Sox had no pitching and Johnny got the blame. The Yankees went to the seventh game of the World Series and I got a pink slip.

Sure I was surprised at being fired; so was Pesky. You just size it up and move on. I thanked the Yankees for giving me the chance to be manager—a job they never trusted Babe Ruth doing. I didn't trash anyone and got offered a job upstairs, but I wanted to remain on the field, so I joined the Mets as a coach the next year. Pesky never bad-mouthed anyone, either. Never blamed anyone, always accepted responsibility, no matter what. That's why guys like Ted Williams loved him—Johnny was always team-first, himself second.

Of course Johnny's always remembered for October 15, 1946, in Sportsman's Park. I was in the park that day watching my pal Joe Garagiola and the Cardinals play the Red Sox in game 7 of the World Series. What happened in the eighth inning changed history, and Pesky has always been blamed for it. Enos Slaughter's dash from first to home on Harry Walker's hit took everyone by surprise, including Johnny, who took a relay from the centerfielder, his back to the infield, and supposedly hesitated throwing the ball home. It was a crushing way to lose, and Pesky became the scapegoat. But it wasn't wholly his fault—if anything, the centerfielder, Leon Culberson, loafed his throw to him. Yet John's remembered all these years for double-clutching on that play, but he didn't. He never shied away from being blamed, and nobody respected him more than his teammates.

I remember in 1952, we were playing Detroit, which had Virgil Trucks pitching. And Pesky was their new shortstop, just acquired a few weeks earlier. Trucks didn't allow a hit until the sixth, when Phil Rizzuto beat out a grounder over the mound. It was called a hit, but

I'm a sports nut and follow all sports all the time. That's pal Joe Garagiola (far left) and fellow St. Louis Cardinal Stan Musial to my left and Red Schoendienst (behind me) visiting heavyweight champion Joe Louis (center) and wrestling legend Lou Thesz (to Louis's right) with the promoter in front, 1948.

the official scorer, John Drebinger of the *New York Times*, called down to the dugout in the eighth inning to ask Pesky about it. And Pesky told him it was definitely an error, saying he got his finger stuck in the webbing of his new glove and should've had Rizzuto. So Trucks got the no-hitter and afterward went over to thank Pesky. "A lot of guys wouldn't have done what you did," he said.

True, and how many guys would voluntarily bench themselves to benefit a teammate and their team? Two years earlier, the Red Sox were battling us for the pennant and Billy Goodman was going for the batting title. Goodman, who had no set position, played a lot of left field when Williams was hurt. But Ted came back and suddenly there was no place for Goodman, who needed four hundred at-bats to qualify for the batting crown. He needed to play every day in September, but everyone in the Red Sox lineup was hitting, including Pesky, who was a rock at third base that season. But Johnny knew the Red Sox needed Williams in the lineup—and he knew Goodman was within reach of the batting title. So Johnny asked to take himself out of the lineup for the last sixteen games so Goodman could play third. Because of that, Goodman won the batting title at .354.

The Yankee Way

Truth is, the biggest motivation was to be the best. To help each other become the best. . . . Overall, our Yankee teams never worried much about the competition; we worried about ourselves.

WHEN YOU JOIN A team for the first time, you don't forget because you always remember. Over sixty years ago, the New York Yankees called me up from the Newark Bears, their top minor-league team. I was just twenty-one, a baby in baseball experience, not wise to what lay ahead. All I knew was there was about a week left in a disappointing 1946 season. It wasn't disappointing to me, it just wasn't good for the Yankees. They had injuries and wartime rustiness and three different managers that season. They would finish in third, seventeen games back, so I guess they thought it couldn't hurt to look at a few minor leaguers.

What did they know about me? I didn't know. I got there the evening before a Sunday double-header against the Philadelphia A's, walking around the stands gazing at the empty stadium, thinking it was like a Grand Canyon for baseball; it was breathtaking and seemed almost sacred. When I walked into the clubhouse, that wasn't shabby, either. It was a large room with nice dressing stalls, Joe DiMaggio's over on the right, near Tommy Henrich's and Charlie Keller's, all those pinstriped uniforms hanging in their lockers. There were a lot of veterans in that room—a lot of pride and tradition, too. It was the same clubhouse Gehrig and Ruth once belonged to.

Did I belong? I really didn't know, but I knew I didn't want to be temporary. Nobody exactly rolled out a red carpet for me and my Newark teammates, Bobby Brown, Vic Raschi, and Frank Colman. I'd already been told I didn't look like a ballplayer, much less a Yankee. Now I was one, at least for a week. All I had ever hoped for was the chance to play professional ball and make a living of it, though I felt that if you liked your work it wasn't really work. Joe Garagiola and I grew up across the street on the Hill, the Italian neighborhood in St. Louis, playing pickup games in empty lots, playgrounds, the streets, wherever. Baseball was our big thing, but the Yankees weren't—Babe Ruth might just as well have been a comic book character. In those days we liked the St. Louis Cardinals and the Browns, and liked the Cardinals a little better because they were. This was the Gashouse Gang—Dizzy Dean and his brother Paul, Pepper Martin, Ducky Medwick, who also happened to be my newspaper customer.

Soon the Yankees would change my life. In 1942, on a tip from my American Legion coach, they signed me for $500—and they hadn't even seen me. After I played a year in Norfolk in the Piedmont League, I did my stint in the navy, training for and participating in the D-day invasion. Coming back to the States, I finished my service at the New London submarine base.

I didn't mind playing a couple of games at third base.
I didn't care where I played as long as I played at all.

I played some ball against service and semipro teams and even an exhibition against the New York Giants. When Mel Ott, their manager, learned I belonged to the Yankees, he called Larry MacPhail and offered $50,000 for me.

MacPhail had just taken over as Yankees president. Since he'd never heard of me, he ordered me to New York to check me out. When I showed up, short and stocky and wearing navy blues, white pants, and a sailor hat, I could tell MacPhail thought I was some-one else. Actually he said I looked like the bottom man on an unemployed acrobatic team. When I later visited the stadium for the first time, I had to convince the workers I was a ballplayer. Pete Sheehy, the clubhouse manager, said I didn't even look like a sailor.

Sheehy had been there since 1926, had seen and known all the greats. But things weren't so great in '46. It was the first season after World War II, and the Yankees veterans had off-years. MacPhail had installed lights at the stadium, and attendance did soar to over two million. But it was a down year otherwise. Guess that's why they wanted to have a look-see at a different-looking guy, which I suppose I was.

Still, I was unknown. Even when I began in Newark in May 1946, I wasn't taken seriously. At first they gave me a raggedy uniform without a number and a cap too small, which didn't thrill me. But I did okay at Newark, playing seventy-seven games and hitting .314 before we lost in the playoffs to the Montreal Royals, which had some pretty good players, including Jackie Robinson. Four months later I was in Yankee Stadium—who'd ever have known?

On the Yankees there's always been tradition by position. Catcher was no different, with Bill Dickey, me, Elston Howard, and Thurman Munson calling games for over fifty years. Here we are in 1977.

When told I'd be catching against the A's on September 22, 1946, I had a few butterflies. I was too new, too nervous to say anything to anybody. Then a guy came over to introduce himself, Spud Chandler. He was a tough-as-nails pitcher and had returned to the Yankees that season after two years in the army. "Kid, don't worry about a thing," he said. "I'm pitching today and I'll take care of you. Just put down anything you want, I'll get it over."

Looking back, this wasn't exactly a religion conversion, but it sure left an impression. A teammate I didn't even know cared about a teammate he didn't know. Chandler was determined to do his job well, so I'd do mine. If my nerves still jangled, they barely did because of him. I hit a home run in my first game and Spud was the winning pitcher, and that didn't feel too bad. I played in seven games at the end of that season, hit .364, and that felt good, too. Felt like I belonged.

Chandler wasn't the first or last guy to ease in a teammate. Still, you can't deny its importance, sixty years ago or today. Joe Mauer of Minnesota, a good young catcher today, once was in the same spot as me, shaking with nerves his very first game. But Brad Radke, a veteran pitcher, told him he'd stick with whatever his catcher called, so don't worry, it's up to him to execute the pitch. Mauer said it was a tremendous confidence boost, and he'd forever remember the impact Radke made on him. Just shows that good team players never go out of style.

Now, 1947 was my rookie season in the majors. It was also Chandler's last, even though he won the ERA title. We had a tremendous club and won the pennant, me playing some outfield because I was still raw as a catcher. As unforgettable years go, '47 belongs in the all-time memory book. Of course, it was the year Jackie broke the color barrier. The year Babe Ruth said his public farewell. It was the first time the World Series was televised. It was also one of the most dramatic Yankee-Brooklyn Series ever. There were big plays, like Al Gionfriddo's spectacular catch on DiMaggio. And there was big heartbreak, like Bill Bevens losing a no-hitter—and the game—with two outs in the ninth inning on Cookie Lavagetto's double. I happened to hit the first pinch homer in World Series history, but if we'd lost I'd have been fitted for goat horns. By the fourth game, the Dodgers had stolen seven bases so Bucky Harris took me out. If I'd thrown out Gionfriddo stealing in game 3, Bevens would've had the no-hitter and the victory.

Maybe I was too confident. Before, the Series reporters asked if I was worried about Jackie and the Dodgers running on me. Nope, I reminded them, Jackie never stole on me in Montreal in the International League. Later that was an important lesson. Never give an opponent added motivation. Now I was feeling bad, but my teammates told me to keep positive. Bevens was in tears after the game and blamed only himself. Any pitcher who walks ten, he said, was living on borrowed time. Chandler also cheered me up, telling me I was too good and too important to get down on myself. We're the Yankees, nobody blames nobody, he said. We need you as much as the other twenty-four guys.

So in game 6 I was back in the lineup, playing right field in front of 74,065, the biggest crowd in Series history. We won the Series in seven, one of the true greatest moments of my life. So began a joyous celebration of teammates, veterans like DiMaggio and George McQuinn, rookies like myself, Bobby Brown, and Spec Shea, and never could I've imagined I'd be destined for so many more.

Before the next season, Spud Chandler retired. His thirty-nine-year-old arm was gone. But I've never forgotten how he helped me. Later I learned how truly dedicated he was to his team, how guys like him helped make the Yankees the Yankees, always there to give a bounce of confidence to a teammate.

Spud didn't make the majors until he was thirty. He was a football player in college, University of Georgia. But pure determination earned him a job with the Yankees in the late 1930s. That's when the Yankees had stars like DiMaggio and Gehrig and Red Ruffing and were winning four straight championships.

In all his years with the Yankees, Chandler would do anything to help his club—starting or relieving. He completed 109 of his 184 career starts. Bill Dickey said he was the most self-assured pitcher he ever caught. Toughest, too. When Spud got injured early in his career, he pitched with bone chips in his arm and never complained—even when he couldn't raise his arm to knot his tie.

In 1943, right before he went in the service, Spud was the league's MVP, going 20–4 with a 1.64 ERA. Dickey said Spud was always pushing the other pitchers, always helping. In 1947 we acquired Allie Reynolds, who was just a mediocre pitcher with Cleveland. But Spud kept encouraging him to be a better pitcher. "Don't just throw the ball," he'd say. "Think about what you're doing. Change speeds. Set hitters up. Think, think, think." I think Allie listened, because he won nineteen games that year and soon became our ace.

That was the Yankee culture I grew up in. That was the character and personality of those teams. Sure the Yankees had stars then, have stars today, and probably always will have stars. But the trademark of great teams is having great team guys: pulling for and helping each other, playing the game right, blending into a team.

Don't get me wrong. Not every guy who joins the Yankees gets eased in by a Spud Chandler, or buys into the team thing. Like they say, you got to earn the pinstripes. As long as I ever knew, new guys were basically told: do the best job you can and we'll help you. After my first couple of games, we were waiting at the 125th Street station for a train to Boston. And DiMaggio kept looking at me, maybe because I didn't look like the classic Yankee that he was. Finally, he kind of laughed, and I laughed right back. "I can hit homers, too," I said. DiMag was great, the greatest I ever played with. Nobody had greater influence on his teammates—he was so determined, totally dedicated. He could be a little distant, but everyone felt his presence. He'd give you a glare if you did something you shouldn't. Being a Yankee and having the proper attitude was real important to him.

People forget what he meant to younger players. When Phil Rizzuto came up, he was only twenty-two, and some of the older guys shunned him. That's because Phil played shortstop, where Frank Crosetti was still entrenched. Then in spring training, DiMag said, "Listen, guys, if this kid is going to play short for us this year, we'd better give him a chance." And Crosetti, as true an organization man as ever was—he spent thirty-six years in the Yankee uniform as player and coach—agreed with DiMag. Give the little fella a chance, he said, and they did. And Phil became a Hall of Famer and probably my closest teammate and friend.

Whenever someone mentions a teammate, I think of different things. Once I was asked to play a game of name association, and someone said, "Mickey Mantle." And I said, what about him?

What could I say about Mickey? Nobody could do the things he did. He ran as fast as any man I ever saw. Had a rocket for an arm and hit moon shots for home runs. But I'll tell you nobody was a better teammate, either. That's what he always wanted as his epitaph: "A Great Teammate." Believe me, there's a reason Tom Tresh and Clete Boyer and others named their kids after Mickey. As a teammate, he was the best.

"Mickey was a god among his teammates," Jim Bouton once said. "I remember on payday, when the traveling secretary brought our checks to the clubhouse, guys would wave the checks and say, 'Thanks, Mick.'"

Mickey was fun to be around, and nobody cheered more for his teammates than he did. He loved sharing jokes and keeping you loose. When we were down three games to one to the Braves in the 1958 World Series, Mickey came into the clubhouse with one of those trick arrows that looked like it came through his head. It cracked everyone up. Probably relaxed us, too, because we won the next three games.

Playing crippled like he did was also inspiring. Guys were amazed what he could do despite all the pain and injuries. My locker was next to his, and each day he'd wrap his legs like a mummy. With damaged knees he'd steal a base if we needed. If he was a superstar, he never acted like it to his teammates. Sure, he had all that ballyhoo when he came up in 1951. And sure, he took every failure hard, he smashed watercoolers and all those things. But nobody wanted to win more, and nobody was a more considerate teammate. If the Yankees won and Mickey went 0-for-4 and struck out every time, he'd still be the gladdest guy in the room.

He had that winning attitude, made every teammate feel important. All of us welcomed Elston Howard when he joined us in 1955 as the team's first black player. To us it wasn't a big deal. For Ellie, it wasn't easy, though. There was still a lot of racism around in the country. He couldn't stay with us at the same hotel in Florida during spring training. So me, Phil Rizzuto, Moose Skowron, and Hank Bauer did everything to include Ellie in activities away from the ballpark. Early that season a bunch of us were eating breakfast at a hotel in Chicago, and Ellie hesitated coming over. So Hank called him over and said, "You play with us, you eat with us. You're one of us."

And he was. Yet Ellie always said he truly felt accepted as a Yankee the day after he hit a triple in the ninth inning to beat Detroit. That's when Mickey lined up a carpet of towels from his locker to the shower. And Mickey was the one heading up the guard of honor. "When he did that I figured I was really part of this team," Ellie said.

Stuff like that is intangible. It shows appreciation, it builds confidence. And let me tell you, you need confidence in sports or whatever you do. Face it, baseball can be a tough, uneasy game. Bottom line, players need the trust and respect of their teammates. When I look back, I wouldn't have gotten some of my positive attitude were it not for guys like Spud Chandler and Joe DiMaggio and Bill Dickey, who came out of retirement to help me, and later Ellie Howard, who once said, "Without Bill, I'm nobody, nobody at all. He made me a catcher." To me that's what the Yankees represented. They always had someone who taught you, advised you, helped you.

There's a lot of instances—Jerry Coleman, for example. Before he came up in 1949, he was a skinny, no-great-shakes infielder whom nobody took real seriously. He had to drink beer to put on weight. Plus he barely hit his weight even after the beers. After the '49 season, Jerry figured he'd give himself one more year and if he couldn't improve out of the minors, he'd quit and learn a business. Well, Jerry made the team in '49, and then Snuffy Stirnweiss, our regular second baseman, got hurt the second game of the year. Jerry really didn't know the position, so he peppered Stirnweiss with questions every day, and Snuffy helped all he could. Stirnweiss helped enough to help Jerry become Rookie of the Year; he and Phil Rizzuto became the smoothest double-play combo in the league, and we won the first of our five straight championships. Jerry was serious, driven, always pep-talking himself at the plate and in the field, always building his own confidence because others had their doubts. I remember when we were celebrating after that '49 Series, Jerry said to Casey Stengel, "Thanks for giving me the chance to play, Skipper. I hope I never disappoint you."

The Ol' Professor telling some amazing stories at a Yankees reunion. Top row: Allie Reynolds, Jim Turner, Joe DiMaggio, Vic Raschi, Tommy Henrich, and Bill Dickey. Bottom row: Phil Rizzuto and me.

He never did. The very next season, Casey brought up Billy Martin, who'd played for him in the minors and was one of his favorites. Billy was only twenty-two, tough and cocky, and thought he should be starting second baseman right away. As Casey said, "There ain't nothing he don't think he can do." But Jerry pulled him aside one day and said, "Look, I know you're going to take my job one day, but there's still things you can't do. Let me help you." And Billy was always talking to Jerry and shadowing him in practice, until 1952, when Jerry was drafted in the Korean War. That's when Billy became the regular at second. It's also when everyone started calling him "Billy the Kid," because he was scrappy and getting into tussles with opponents. Billy wasn't the defensive player Jerry was, but he had the same alertness and smarts, and that's what saved the '52 World Series for us. In game 7 against Brooklyn, Jackie Robinson hit a bases-loaded pop-up that our first baseman, Joe Collins, lost in the sun. Suddenly Billy came dashing in all the way and made a game-saving lunging grab. As he did, he immediately pulled the ball out of his glove and squeezed with his bare hand, so he wouldn't drop it if someone collided with him.

Billy always credited Jerry for helping him be a big-leaguer. That was Jerry, doing whatever to help the Yankees win, caring about his teammates. In 1956, after we won the World Series, Enos Slaughter was supposed to get only a half share of the winners' take. Enos was forty and had misplayed a couple of balls against Brooklyn. To be honest, he wasn't the most popular guy among the Yankees. He'd played almost his whole career with the Cardinals. He was a rah-rah guy and we weren't a rah-rah team. Plus he hadn't been with us that long. But he'd never made much money in baseball, and he was a key contributor after we got him in August. Jerry and a number of guys thought Slaughter should get a fairer share. That's when Jerry went to the commissioner and requested that Slaughter be raised to a three-quarter share. Ford Frick, the commissioner, agreed, and Slaughter got over $6,000, which he sure appreciated.

When we traded Billy in '57, Jerry showed his class again. Now he was helping Bobby Richardson, who along with Tony Kubek was the future double-play combo. As Kubek said, "Bobby and I were astonished that Jerry Coleman and Gil McDougald went out of their way to help us, for we were to ultimately take their jobs. It was typical of the Yankee pinstripe loyalty. There was always an atmosphere of helping on the club—the Mantles, the McDougalds, the Careys, the Colemans were eager to help out. They had been through it and they were there to show us the way."

I tried my best to live up to this tradition, helping younger guys and teammates whenever I could, passing along whatever tips I could. Especially in spring training, when we'd bring in six or seven catchers every year. Obviously we couldn't keep them all, so I was glad to see when guys like Clint Courtney, Lou Berberet, and Gus Triandos found work on other teams, hoping in some way that I'd helped them out.

The great Yankees teams were always about the team first. How else can I say it? It's no secret that almost anybody joining the Yankees had to be intimidated. Hard to imagine how they couldn't. But I always heard stories about how the greats always helped the young guys settle down, like Chandler with me. Bill Dickey told me that when he came up in 1928, he was having trouble hitting big-league pitching. In fact, he was getting scared. Then Lou Gehrig took him aside and said, "I think I can help you with your hitting." Dickey was surprised because most veterans didn't really talk to rookies much. But Gehrig worked with him several days—he was uppercutting on the ball—and straightened him out. They later became roommates and best buddies, and Dickey said he always wondered what might've happened if Gehrig hadn't taken that interest.

My buddy Phil Rizzuto was always a Nervous Nellie. His first game in Yankee Stadium in 1941 was real unsettling until Lefty Gomez called him to the mound. Lefty asked Phil if his mother was in the stands. Then Gomez told Phil to stand there next to him and he'd make her proud, "because now she thinks her little boy is giving advice to the great Gomez."

One of the most nervous guys joining the Yankees was Moose Skowron. Seems strange since he was a big and tough football player at Purdue. He came up through the Yankee system, starting as a third baseman, until Casey Stengel told him he'd better learn to play first if he wanted to make the majors. He even sent him to dancing school to improve his footwork. When Moose came up to the Yankees in 1954, he was shy, nervous, and insecure. We'd just won our fifth straight World Series. Joe Collins was our regular first baseman. And Pete Sheehy, our equipment man, gave Moose uniform No. 53—not a good sign he'd stick, since few players wore numbers in the '50s. But in spring training, Collins put his arm around Moose and told him, "Look, I'll pull for you when you're playing. And hopefully you'll pray for me when I'm playing." I know Moose appreciated that, but he was still not entirely sure he belonged. At that time I didn't have a roommate and asked Moose to room with me. But he politely said a rookie shouldn't room with a veteran. Moose was serious; he never knew when guys were kidding, and I wasn't kidding.

As a rookie, Moose didn't even have his own bats and was too intimidated to speak up. Seeing this, Hank Bauer told him to go ahead and use his bats. Moose did and hit a couple in the upper deck at Comiskey Park. Believe me, Moose thought the world of Hank after that. The next year, when Ellie Howard joined us in spring training, it was Moose who picked him up at the train station. They'd been teammates in the minors, and Ellie appreciated being welcomed to the majors by a familiar face. After the '55 season we went on a goodwill tour to Japan, and Ellie and Moose roomed together. To Moose it was no big deal, even if interracial roommates didn't happen in those days. They were friends and teammates, and on the Yankees your teammate was also a friend.

Hank would always look out for Moose. And Moose would always do anything for anybody. He was a good ballplayer and hardworking, and he never complained, except maybe if Casey pinch-hit for him in the first inning, which he actually did. When Moose was hitting .300 every year, Hank finally convinced him he was underpaid. He told him he didn't realize how important he was to the team. Back then the Yankees front office could be pretty coldhearted. Every contract was a struggle. You didn't like what you got offered? Tough luck. The salaries weren't much, maybe $15,000–$20,000 in those days. There was no free agency then; the owners had the power. The players were like cows in the pasture. Your team was your family—and you helped and depended on each other.

Up until the day Hank died, he and Moose were closest pals. For years they ran a Yankees fantasy camp together and were always helping each other. A few years ago, we had an event for Yankee first basemen at our museum and Moose flew in overnight wearing a shirt with the monogram "H.B." Moose just said he had no more clean shirts so he borrowed Hank's.

Nobody didn't like or respect Hank Bauer. He was hard-nosed and fearless, but friendly, too. He had four years of combat duty with the marines in the Pacific, and some of us called him the "Bruiser" because he played all out all the time. Hank was one of the twelve Yankees who played on all five straight championship (1949–1953) teams. He burned about not playing every day, but Casey platooned him with Gene Woodling. Platooning was unusual then. Set lineups were normal. But Casey made platooning an advantage, figuring two players of equal ability—one right-handed, one left-handed—were more effective than one player. He figured he'd get better results from a combo of two players, and he did. Both Hank and Woodling were hardly thrilled about not playing regularly. But as Casey said, "They complain about it, but they go to the bank every winter."

Hank took the game dead serious; so did Woodling. While they both fussed at Casey, it was nothing personal. It was all about winning—both wanted to win real bad. Frank Crosetti used to call them "you two dumb squareheads," but everyone respected the hell out of them. Hank was almost always first at the ballpark and last to leave. He expected you to hustle and be as serious at the game as him. I'm not sure if he actually told Moose, "Don't mess with my money," but that was the famous saying Hank used all the time. Meaning, if you were new on the Yankees, you better not screw up because we're counting on our World Series shares.

No question, money was partly a motivation for us in those days. Most of our team could make about half their salary by winning the World Series. And Hank had some sensational Series, especially in 1951 against the Giants, which had all the momentum after beating the Dodgers for the pennant on Bobby Thomson's famous home run. But as Red Smith, one of my favorite newspaper guys in our day, wrote after that Series, "Magic and sorcery and incantation and spells had taken the Giants to the championship of the National League and put them into the World Series. But you don't beat the Yankees with a witch's broomstick. Not the Yankees, not when there's hard money to be won."

The money was important, I won't kid you. Back then we all worked in the off-season, so the extra cash helped. Truth is, though, the biggest motivation was to be the best. To help each other become the best. I always felt part of my job was to study the hitters, keep a mental book. Also, I had to know my pitchers, know what stuff worked and what didn't. Once we had a cocky young pitcher who told me how a certain hitter couldn't hit curveballs. I told him maybe he couldn't hit Eddie Lopat's or Whitey Ford's curveball, but how do you know he couldn't hit yours? To me, too many pitchers thought they knew too much. I wanted them to make sure they made the most of their skills, but be aware of their limits.

Overall, our Yankees teams never worried much about the competition; we worried about ourselves. Didn't matter if it was the Indians with their great pitching staff or those great Brooklyn teams we faced in the World Series, we didn't go out to try to beat somebody; we went out to play the very best we could. Like I said, I always tried helping my pitcher not to think, just pitch.

People try to make winning a science, but it isn't. It's simple. You want to win, you try like heck to win, that's it. It's like Herm Edwards tried to explain when he was coaching the Jets a few years ago, "You *play* to *win* the *game*." On our teams, every starter or scrubeenie was bent on winning by doing their part. I heard someone say once, "If you do more than you're paid to do, you'll eventually be paid more for what you do." That was basically our feeling about winning.

When people ask me what it was like being part of ten world championships, I say I was lucky. I was born at the right time. I also think our team unity and determination set us apart. Guys on the Yankees supported and trusted each other—that was the Yankee way. In the train, the hotel, the clubhouse, we'd talk baseball for hours. And we had fun together. Ever hear about "twenty-five guys, twenty-five cabs," meaning guys going on their own in their own way? You never heard it about the Yankees.

Who made the Yankee tradition thing a big thing? I think a lot had to do with Joe McCarthy. He was obsessed with fundamentals. His teams never beat themselves. He took over as manager in the early 1930s and quit early in '46, so I never played for him. But when I came up, there was a Yankee way of doing things, a Yankee image because of McCarthy. Mostly, he was about acting professional. He was about the little things, which add up to big things. Because of him, guys always had to wear jackets and ties. His idea was to build self-respect and pride. "You're Yankees—act like Yankees," McCarthy said.

That's a big reason the Yankees got that image they still have today. They're all business, they respect the tradition. The pinstripes, the monuments, the stadium, that's all part of it. But more important is the confidence, the atmosphere of teamwork. Players change, but the respect and expectations don't. No facial hair or long hair? No problem for Johnny Damon. Calling his manager "Mister" is no big thing for Derek Jeter.

McCarthy was serious and demanding, but the players respected him. How couldn't they? It's like Joe Torre today. There was a confidence about his teams. Every player had a confident attitude, McCarthy made sure of it. He didn't invent pinstripes, but he cared about the image—he promoted that whole power mystique, the Bronx Bombers. Bill Dickey told me his teams wore squarer caps because McCarthy thought it made the players look tougher. McCarthy was sort of ahead of his time. He insisted on his players being in excellent physical condition. Who doesn't do conditioning year-round nowadays? McCarthy split his staff into starters and relievers in 1936, the first guy to use a relief specialist. Nowadays how can you play without one?

If McCarthy questioned your commitment, you were out the door. In 1937, the Yankees lost two straight to Detroit, and McCarthy was pretty upset. An outfielder named Roy Johnson asked, "What does McCarthy want?" When McCarthy heard about Johnson's question, he got rid of him, saying, "That man is not sufficiently into winning."

It kind of reminded me of when Ruben Sierra, a pretty good ballplayer, criticized Joe Torre, complaining that all the Yankees cared about was winning. Sierra was unloaded, too, before he realized he'd made a mistake and was later brought back.

I don't like to compare, but it's not unfair to compare Joe McCarthy with Joe Torre. Each guided a Yankee dynasty with the same style. Each preached teamwork. Each instilled his own kind of discipline, each earned great respect, and respect means everything on any team. You better respect your boss, and he should respect you, too. McCarthy never criticized a guy in public. Players respected that. Neither does Torre. If they had a problem, they'd tell you privately. Even with stars like Gehrig and DiMaggio, who were McCarthy's two favorite players, his rules applied to all.

That's not so true nowadays. So many coaches coddle their stars, even high school and college coaches. They give them more leeway than other players.

Sometimes that's not good for team spirit, especially if the guy is too individualistic. Back in my day, DiMaggio had more money and influence than any of us. But selfish he wasn't. All DiMag cared about was the team. In 1949, he was hurt bad, missed three months with those heel spurs that didn't respond to surgery. But he surprised everyone when he played in a big July series in Boston. It was like a storybook—he hit four homers and drove in nine runs those three games, and even the fans in Fenway gave him a standing ovation. His comeback was all people talked about, and *Life* magazine put him on the cover. But all the attention DiMag didn't care for. He was just satisfied he could help us win, and that's simply all he said.

The Red Sox caught up to us that season. It didn't help that we had a heap of injuries, I think seventy-seven in all. Besides DiMag being out, I had a broken thumb, Henrich fractured his back; we were a patchwork team all year. All the Red Sox needed was to win one of the last two games in Yankee Stadium for the pennant. The first game happened to be Joe DiMaggio Day, when he was honored before the game and told everyone, "I want to thank my fans, my friends, my manager, Casey Stengel, my teammates; the gamest fightingest bunch of guys that ever lived. And I want to thank the Good Lord for making me a Yankee." As it happened, Joe had pneumonia, looked weak and underweight, and was still limping around. Even his brother Dom told his Red Sox teammates that he didn't see how Joe could play, but he did.

When he played hurt, how could anyone complain? It rallied guys together. DiMag gave you that confidence just to be on the field with him. Whatever he did was all team-based. It's hard to remember him making a mistake on the field. And he never got thrown out of a game his whole career. That last game on October 2, 1949, was a sudden-death situation, and we were ahead 5–0 in the ninth inning. But Raschi was tiring, and DiMag couldn't reach Bobby Doerr's triple to right center—if healthy, he probably would've caught it. Realizing he might be hurting the team, he called time and took himself out of the game.

Sure DiMag was special. Heck, he was the best ballplayer in the game. He drove in 155 runs and almost single-handedly carried us in '48. Yet when Casey took over as manager in 1949, he didn't want stars—he wanted the star to be the team. But he handled DiMag with understanding, allowing him to judge when he should or shouldn't play.

Great players, if they're really great players, should have that influence. After the '46 season, the Yankees were looking to get a pitcher and consulted DiMag. He urged them to get Allie Reynolds, who was only 11–15 from Cleveland, so they got him. And Reynolds would always thank DiMag for helping rescue his career.

Baseball is not basketball, but DiMaggio to us was kind of like Michael Jordan to his team. He was the biggest star around, an honest-to-goodness perfectionist. Both pushed themselves and their teammates to play as hard as they could. I got to know Jordan at charity golf events. He called me "Mr. B" (I don't remember calling him Mr. J because I also played with Dr. J, who was Julius Erving), and I'm glad I didn't anger Jordan, which I once did DiMaggio at the American Airlines classic when I actually hit him with one of my drives.

No question Jordan is hypercompetitive, even in golf. Like DiMag, his intensity rubbed off on everyone around him. Both had an aura, dressed in the best suits I could never have; both were sort of intimidating. Yet what really set them apart, besides their supreme talent, was their dignity, grace, and loyalty to their team.

There are teams, and there are great teams. Great teams like those Chicago Bulls teams had Jordan, but they got the most out of each guy. Forget Jordan's amazing skill and highlight dunks. Pushing and pushing his teammates to be the best is one of the things he did. They say basketball is more of an individualistic sport than the others. But Jordan knew he needed his teammates to win, and I know some didn't care for his criticism. If he was rough on them to work harder, to play smarter, the results are the results. The Bulls won six championships in his last six seasons. "Talent wins games," he once said, "but teamwork and intelligence wins championships."

DiMag knew it, too. He expected—demanded—that you play as hard and smart as him. In my rookie year, Joe Page was one of our real hard-throwing pitchers, but real fun-loving, too. He'd stay out late often, and his pitching got erratic. Then DiMag made him his road roommate and laid into him about wasting his talent. Since this was coming from DiMag, he listened good and shaped up good. He was the best reliever in the league for four years.

Mostly DiMag gave younger guys a winning attitude. He'd take rookies out to dinner, make you feel like you belong, but he always expected you to play right, no mistakes. Spec Shea was a happy-go-lucky pitcher who roomed with me as a rookie in 1947; we stayed at the Edison Hotel, where DiMag also stayed and would buy us breakfast. Spec always said DiMag made him feel confident—he'd tell him, don't worry about guys hitting it in the air, he'd catch it. Once DiMag got a little mad at him because Spec said he was going to pitch a guy inside, so our infield and outfield would shift. But Spec pitched outside and nobody was in the right position. When Spec told him the ball got away from him, DiMag didn't buy it. Told him he was in the major leagues, and you can't make those mistakes or we won't win.

Make no mistake, that's what DiMag did; he made you better. Spec won fourteen games his rookie year, made the All-Star team, and won two games in the World Series. One of my favorite pictures in our museum is DiMag hugging Spec after winning game 5 against the Dodgers in the '47 Series.

Good teams do good because they have people who enjoy seeing others succeed. To me that's part of the brilliance of Jordan and DiMag—they lifted the level of play of everyone else. When DiMag retired, he always said his greatest thrill wasn't his fifty-six-game hitting streak, it was being part of nine championship teams.

When a team's best player shows loyalty to his teammates, it's a contagious thing. The team takes on the attributes of that best player. Every team is molded to maximize the talents of individuals—what team isn't? But individuals can create a team spirit, like LaDainian Tomlinson does with the San Diego Chargers. Sure he's the best runner. And he's always showing his teammates he cares about them. On the play before he broke the NFL scoring record, he told everyone in the huddle to join him in the end zone. After the game he thanked the defense, special teams, and coaches and said, "If wasn't for the team, there wouldn't be any record."

To me one of the greatest records ever was Lou Gehrig's iron-man streak. Despite back pain, bad colds, spike wounds, fractured fingers, and who knows what other ailments, he played in 2,130 straight games. Of course, his teammates respected him enormously, and why wouldn't they? He played through every injury. Did everything you could do on a ballfield, a team guy by example. Besides all his home runs, he hit a bunch of triples and stole home a number of times; he even laid down twenty-one sacrifice bunts on those famous 1927 Yankees, Murderer's Row. He was low-key and shy, overshadowed on his own team by Ruth, then later DiMaggio, but to him it didn't matter. His allegiance was always to his team, even if he didn't really socialize with his teammates except for Dickey. Those great Yankees teams in the '30s were a bunch of tobacco-chewing, tough-guy characters, and Gehrig wasn't.

Dickey told me Gehrig was proud of being captain. Even when he got ill, and announced his retirement early in 1939, he stayed with the team and took the lineup to the umpires. When they say Gehrig was the ultimate team player, it's hard to argue. In his famous "luckiest man" speech, he thanks his old and current teammates. He knew he was fortunate to play with guys who cared as much as him.

Dickey told me nobody admired Gehrig more than Joe McCarthy, his manager, who felt he was everything a professional should be, serious and efficient. Back in those days, McCarthy banned shaving in the clubhouse, because he expected guys to be clean-shaven when they got to work. He banned card games, too. "This is a clubhouse, not a club room. I want players to think of baseball and nothing else."

Actually, that wasn't always so. Dickey, Henrich, DiMaggio, Joe Gordon, and Lefty Gomez and those guys had their fun. They played bridge on the train (McCarthy wouldn't let them play poker), went out in New York together, and needled each other about playing the hardest, since McCarthy would've reminded them otherwise.

But McCarthy won them over. The Yankees worked and worked on fundamentals. Mental mistakes were inexcusable. But his players responded pretty good; four straight championships (1936–1939) ain't too bad. Guys had no problem shifting positions if it'd help the team—Red Rolfe, a shortstop, changed into a third baseman so Frank Crosetti could play short, and Joe Gordon, another shortstop, was moved to second.

Henrich used to tell how McCarthy kept promoting team harmony. Once McCarthy was talking to writers before a game and said, "I'll show you a team player," and called to Gordon to come over. "So Joe," he asked his All-Star second baseman, "what's your batting average?"

Gordon: "I don't know."

McCarthy: "What are you fielding?"

Gordon: "I don't know."

McCarthy turned to the writers and said, "That's what I like. All he does is come to beat you."

Things don't happen without a cause, because they just don't. DiMaggio and Henrich, who both came up on those Yankees teams, were my early teammates and the most loyal team guys I'd ever know. In 1941, I was sixteen and playing American Legion ball for the Stockham Post. We were a good amateur team and traveled all around, and people everywhere were caught up in the excitement of DiMaggio's hitting streak. Years later Rizzuto (who was a rookie then) told me how every guy on the Yankees felt sheer joy in sharing in it.

When DiMag reached thirty-seven, still a few games short of George Sisler's major league record, it looked like it might be over. He was hitless with the Yankees leading in the eighth inning. DiMag was up fourth that inning. With a runner on and one out, Henrich was up. He immediately figured there's no guarantee DiMag would get to bat. What if he lined into a double play? So Henrich asked McCarthy if it'd be okay for him to sacrifice. And McCarthy thought it over, then nodded okay. Henrich sacrificed, DiMag cracked a double, and the streak continued. That to me was Tommy Henrich. He always came through. Always came through in the clutch on the field, was always there to help a team-mate. When he quit, he worked long, hard hours to help Mickey Mantle learn playing outfield. Everybody always respected Tommy.

In a lot of ways, Henrich was one of the truest Yankees. He was a straight shooter, tough, serious, clean-cut, and a gentleman. I was his teammate at the end of his career, but nobody was prouder of the Yankee tradition that went back to Babe Ruth's era.

And that's where it all started. The Babe changed baseball forever. He's the greatest Yankee ever. After all these years he's still a mythic hero. I only met him once, when I was a rookie in 1947. It was in Sportsman's

Park in St. Louis, part of his farewell tour of all the ballparks. He wasn't in the best of health, but he was friendly, even posed for a picture with me when someone asked him. Even today I regret not asking for his autograph—I'm sure I was too awestruck.

Babe started the Yankee tradition. He's still the greatest. So much has been written and said about him, or as Waite Hoyt, one of his teammates, used to say, "Even the lies about him are true." Hoyt was a great pitcher, a high-class guy, and later a broadcaster. He knew Babe as good as anyone, knew all about his flamboyance and overeating, overdrinking, and overdoing everything. Once he was telling me stories about the Babe and stressed how he was one heck of a teammate, loyal to the end. In the 1932 World Series, he criticized the Cubs for shortchanging his friend and former teammate Mark Koenig on his World Series share. When the Cubs razzed him back, Babe hit his famous "called shot" home run. He loved to put on a show and have a good time, but he was there to win and his teammates loved him. Of course, Babe helped make them extra money by barnstorming until he got in trouble. His real trouble was he never liked anyone telling him what to do. That's why he got into run-ins with the commissioner (Judge Landis) and his manager (Miller Huggins) and even had a misunderstanding with Gehrig. But he was always team-minded and resolved almost all his spats. Including one with Hoyt, who didn't speak to him for a year because he thought he'd dogged a fly ball. A year earlier, Babe had gotten into a dugout fight with Wally Pipp, because he'd criticized his play at first base. No, things were never dull with Babe. Ironically,

Pipp would be replaced by Gehrig at first, and he later became Babe's ghostwriter.

Speaking of ghosts, and curses, I don't believe in them. What I know is that Ruth started making the Yankees the greatest franchise in sports. Every kid today knows the name Babe Ruth. His performance and personality really became the Yankees.

And I know that what Babe said a long time ago is maybe truer today than ever. "The way a team plays as a whole determines its success," he said. "You may have the greatest bunch of individual stars in the world, but if they don't play together, the club won't be worth a dime."

Catching Perfection

I always count catching Don Larsen's perfect game in the '56 World Series as probably the best [thrill]. . . . As remarkable as Don pitched that day, the perfect game is also testament to the team. Success doesn't happen without everyone pulling together.

WHEN PEOPLE ASK ME my greatest thrill, I say, which one? I've had so many, and so many I don't even remember. Of course I always count catching Don Larsen's perfect game in the '56 World Series as probably the best. Over a hundred years they've been playing the World Series, and it'd never happened before and it's never happened since.

To be part of it, to help make it true, it's still a heck of a feeling. What makes it a greater experience is its being a shared experience. Don pitched it, we all shared in it. It was historic, but more important, it was *real* important. Don shut down the Brooklyn Dodgers in a crucial game, putting us up 3–2 in the Series. You know, honestly, that was the biggest thing. A lot of us didn't even realize it was a *perfect* game until afterward.

Part of all the hoopla around Don Larsen was because it was Don Larsen. A guy nobody would've ever imagined to pitch the greatest game in history. They said he was supposed to be a bad boy, an underperformer. Two years earlier he was 3–21 with the Baltimore Orioles. Two of those wins came against us, and the next year he came to us in that big eighteen-player trade. Larsen had a good arm. He liked having a good time, too. During spring training in '56, he crashed into a telephone pole at 5 A.M. We heard George Weiss, our general manager, wanted to trade him right then. But Casey shrugged it off with his usual line that Larsen was probably out mailing a letter.

Don was mostly our fourth starter that season. Some guys called him "Night Rider," and others called him "Gooney Bird," since he was tall and gangly. He pitched good in September, using a new no-windup delivery, which wasn't done in those days. He adopted it because he thought he'd been tipping off his pitches.

Unfortunately he didn't get many pitches over in game 2. Larsen was so wild that Casey yanked him in the second inning. We had a 6–0 lead, but Don walked four and gave up four runs and we lost, 13–8. Larsen was real disgusted with himself.

In those days the World Series happened quick. No travel days. We played every day. No time to dwell on anything. I'm sure Don didn't think he'd ever pitch for Casey again.

I remember driving to Yankee Stadium for game 5 trying to think what Casey was thinking. Who was he going to pitch? Who'd be in the lineup? I did know Maglie was going to be tough to beat. He was thirty-nine, real wise, with three different types of curveballs. He had beaten us in game 1 and had just thrown a no-hitter two weeks earlier.

Our clubhouse was quiet before the game. We learned of our starting pitcher when Frank Crosetti walked over to Larsen's locker and placed the ball in his shoe. Meanwhile, Casey was still playing around with the lineup, shuffling it like a deck of cards. Andy Carey, our third baseman, was struggling, so Casey was thinking of putting Billy Hunter at shortstop and moving Gil McDougald, our regular shortstop, to third. He couldn't decide until the last minute.

As it turned out, both Carey and McDougald made a big difference. Jackie Robinson hit a hard smash that ricocheted off Carey's glove to McDougald, who got Jackie by a step. It was only in the second inning. Who knew it'd be a famous play?

Over forty years later, me and Don were at the stadium when they had a special day for me. That was when David Cone pitched his perfect game. It was an unforgettable achievement, but David always credited his teammates. "There were great plays throughout the day. Scottie Brosius made a great play, Paul O'Neill, Chuck Knoblauch . . . I think everybody feels good about this because everybody can say, 'You know, I did something today to help this come true.'"

Truthfully, I didn't realize until the sixth or seventh inning that Larsen hadn't given up a hit. My concentration was really on winning the game. We were only up 2–0, and I'd been through a bad no-hitter experience in the World Series before. My rookie year, 1947, I was catching Bill Bevens against Brooklyn in Ebbets Field in game 4. Bevens had walked ten but was one out from a no-hitter and a 2–1 victory. And he would've had it if I'd thrown out Al Gionfriddo trying to steal second with two outs. But he beat my throw, and Bucky Harris, our manager, ordered an intentional walk to Pete Reiser to face Cookie Lavagetto, a pinch hitter. We threw him a high outside fastball, just like the scouting report said, but he hit it for a double to win the game. Bevens felt awful. I remember him crying in the clubhouse. The biggest hurt was over losing the game, not the no-hitter.

Nine years later, I wasn't worried about anybody's immortality. None of us were. With the shadows creeping over the stadium in the late innings, we just wanted to finish the job. Looking back, I'm not real sure what transformed Don that day. Maybe it was because he'd gotten the hell beaten out of him three days earlier. Whatever it was, he was extra sharp all afternoon. I liked his fastball best and called for it most. He had a good slider and the best control I'd ever seen. Everything I put down, he got over. He never shook me off and was ahead of every hitter, except Pee Wee Reese in the first. Don gave me a lot of credit afterward, saying I did all his thinking for him.

He credited all of us for playing perfect behind him. A perfect game doesn't happen without skill, luck, and teamwork. All of that happened on October 8, 1956.

When it comes to perfect, Mickey Mantle was a perfectionist or at least real demanding of himself. He always said Larsen's game was the biggest in his life—and he played like it. His home run off Sal Maglie in the fourth was our first hit and a big boost, giving us a lead. And he made that running backhanded catch off Gil Hodges in deep left center, one of the best he ever made.

Mickey was one heck of a teammate, and not only because of what he could do on the field. He had that way of lifting your spirit, of easing tension. But his nerves were jittery that day, like everyone's. In the late innings, we all stayed away from Larsen in the dugout. Nobody wanted to jinx him. As his catcher, I couldn't think of anything to say to help him. He didn't need advice. He needed antacids. By the seventh inning, Don was smoking a cigarette and walked by Mickey and said, "Look at the scoreboard, Mick. Wouldn't it be something?" Mickey told him to shut up and walked past him. In the ninth inning, Mickey later told me, his knees were shaking, and he prayed nobody would hit the ball in his direction.

Just before the ninth, Billy Martin gathered the infielders and reminded them to knock everything down. Nothing gets by nobody.

Before we headed out for the last inning, I said to Larsen, let's get the first out, that's the main thing. On the newsreels you could see how nervous he was, wiping his brow, fidgeting with the rosin bag. I never saw the game in its entirety until fifty years later. A film collector named Doak Ewing had an original copy of the broadcast and showed it at our museum for me and Don and others to see. Man, the game went by fast, only one commercial sponsor, not like today. Mostly Larsen's control and pace made it quick, and Maglie was no molasses, either. The calling of the announcer, Bob Wolff, who was also there with us in the museum, was interesting. He didn't want to jinx Larsen, either. In the late innings he kept avoiding the words "no-hitter" and "perfect game."

Watching it reminded me that baseball's a team game, but it's also man against man, pitcher against batter.

Watching it on TV, you see what kids call a game of catch. It was me and Don, with a guy in between, trying to break up our game. The last batter was Dale Mitchell, who we knew from his days with Cleveland. A good hitter who rarely struck out.

We went with a fastball on a 1–2 pitch, and Dale started to swing but held up. Didn't matter. The ump, Babe Pinielli, called strike three. To this day people say the pitch was high. Maybe, maybe not, but it was a strike. Even Dale admitted later he shouldn't have taken any chances. I jumped into Larsen's arms—it was a tremendous feeling. And Don was still almost numb over what he'd done. The clubhouse was a mad scene. Reporters everywhere, lots of jubilation. Even some of the Dodgers, including the owner, Walter O'Malley, Jackie, and Maglie later came in to congratulate him.

After we won the Series a couple of days later, our equipment manager, Pete Sheehy, took my catcher's mitt and had it bronzed. Today it's in our museum and is one of two remembrances I have from that day. The other is a special plaque that Don personalized and gave to each of his teammates. It has a picture of him throwing the last pitch, with the words:

Presented to Yogi Berra. With sincerest appreciation for your efforts and contribution in accomplishing the First Perfect Game in World Series history. Gratefully, Don Larsen.

All these years later, there's still a supreme fascination with Don's perfect game. It's been written about and talked about and celebrated as much as any game ever played. Some say it was the greatest achievement in American sports. At the least it's right up there. How do you surpass perfection?

Honestly, it's like something out of a storybook. It happened in the greatest stadium against one of the greatest lineups in history. It had never happened before in the World Series, and I can't imagine it ever happening again.

As remarkable as Don pitched that day, the perfect game is also testament to the team. Success doesn't happen without everyone pulling together. And I'll tell you, our teams always did.

Don deserved what happened. He persevered. He rewarded the faith of his manager. He respected his opponent. He raised his game when his teammates needed it most. In turn, they were also tremendous. I had the perfect view.

What Were They Thinking?

Handling frustration and controlling emotions are hugely important on the playing field and off. . . . In the larger picture, you have to be accountable. Is one dumb action worth risking so much?

GROWING UP IN ST. LOUIS, we used to play pickup games in Sublette Park and the empty lot down near my house on Elizabeth Avenue, and we played because we loved it. Our parents couldn't have been more uninvolved if they wanted and they never wanted. This was the 1930s. My pop was from the Old World and never knew American sports, other than it being a waste of time. So me and Joe Garagiola organized a bunch of us into a neighborhood gang, the Stags AC. Actually it was a sports club without uniforms and screaming adults. And we played other gangs. In those days we self-taught ourselves in every sport, chose up sides, set rules, made the games interesting . . . we just had fun.

Today a ten-year-old kid playing sports has probably had a half dozen coaches already. I'm sure they count winning as the big thing and don't count so much on the learning, improving, and enjoying. If I could tell one thing to all the adults involved with these forty million kids who play organized sports today, I'd remind them that youth sports are for youth, not for you. Let them have fun and enjoy their participation. Let mistakes be opportunities to teach. As a parent or a coach, don't let emotions get hold of you. What you say or do has an effect, always remember that. Get a kid fearful about making a mistake, you'll also get a kid who makes excuses or complains. You want kids to care about playing right and enjoying themselves, not dwelling on the winning or losing. Praise and encourage them without being a sideline loudmouth. Kids must be responsible for their own words and actions, too.

It's no easy lesson. Some of the best athletes in the world make terrible decisions, do dumb things. Unfortunately, bad decisions are made because of frayed tempers or frustration. Still, you wonder, what were they thinking?

Being a big soccer fan, I didn't know what to think after watching Zinedine Zidane, France's biggest star, ram his head into that Italian player in the 2006 World Cup. Surely he knew what was at stake. Millions of people watching. Biggest game in the world. So what if the Italian guy taunted him? He lost it. Couldn't control himself, left his team a man down, and they wound up losing.

Great player he is, great team player he wasn't. Not when he let down his teammates, his entire country, only to respond to an insult. But I don't know what surprised me more—that he was forgiven by a majority of French fans or that he apologized but didn't regret what he did. Truth is, he showed weakness when his team needed him to be strong.

Most bad decisions—ones that really mess up things—are made impulsively. When I broke into the major leagues, they'd holler a lot of stuff at me. Opposing players would hang from the dugouts making ape sounds. I was called Neanderthal Man, got razzed about my looks, the way I talked, the things I said. Some of the insults didn't make me feel too good, either. But I just adopted the attitude that what people say about me, that's their opinion. I have to satisfy myself with what I'm doing. It's the same in life as it is in playing ball. If you let something get under your skin, you'll never get the job done.

Trash-talking was a big thing in my day. I heard it all. When the writers said I was knock-kneed, stumpy, a gorilla in flannels, I didn't care. I figured if I was good enough to play for the Yankees, that was good enough. Besides, I always tried to use insults as motivation. And like I said, I never saw anyone hit with his face.

The worst heckling and abuse were for Jackie Robinson and Larry Doby, the first black players who came into the big leagues the same year as me. But they did what they did—ignored everything—so other blacks and minorities could get a chance, too. Being in the American League, I really didn't see what Jackie went through. But I know Larry's treatment was just as brutal. Some of his Cleveland teammates wouldn't even speak to him. And the Philadelphia A's hired a heckler to harass Larry whenever the Indians played there. The guy also traveled to Yankee Stadium to distract him. Finally, the heckler got discouraged because Larry quietly went about his business, played real well in '48, and helped the Indians win the championship.

The heckler approached him and said, "You know, you're a good sport."

I knew Larry Doby a long time and knew he kept a lot inside. I knew he once threatened to get a heckler, and he even got into a brawl against us in 1957. But when it mattered most, he and Jackie Robinson had enough willpower to overcome temptations and emotions. So much was at stake, so much depended on being cool under fire.

There's an old saying, "Count to ten when you're angry." If only more people did it. A bad snap decision can have a bad consequence. My mentor Bill Dickey was a gentleman, quiet, a real team man when he played in the 1930s. Unfortunately, he once lost his temper on a rough play at the plate and broke the guy's jaw with a single punch. He was hitting .360 at the time and was suspended thirty days. "Biggest regret I ever had," he once told me, "because it hurt the whole club."

Handling frustration and controlling emotions, they're hugely important on the playing field and off. One person's actions can affect many people. Juan Marichal always regretted smacking John Roseboro in the head with his bat in 1965. It was a terrible incident, one of the worst ever. It also had a bad impact on Marichal's team, since the Giants were already pitching-thin. Marichal got suspended eight games, and the Giants lost the pennant to the Dodgers by two games.

I'm a big hockey fan from way back. I regularly work out at the Devils' facility and like the players a lot—they're loyal, team-first guys. They're like a family. The sport itself is highly emotional, and teammates always appreciate teammates who back them up in the heat of battle. That's the hockey code. Still, there's no defending what Chris Simon of the Islanders did to the Rangers' Ryan Hollweg in 2007, swinging his stick full-bore at his neck. That was nothing but selfish. It didn't help his team. He did it to get his own personal revenge. He got suspended and the Islanders began losing. Really, what was he thinking?

Everyone has a bad spur of the moment. But it shouldn't result in a serious, lasting consequence. In the larger picture, you have to be accountable. Is one dumb action worth risking so much?

When people ask me the maddest I ever got, it was probably the 1955 World Series. Jackie Robinson stealing home, although he was really out. I knew he was out and he's still out. When the ump, Bill Summers, called him safe, I got pretty livid. But as much as I yelled and squawked, I never cussed Summers. As much as I knew he was out, I also knew I couldn't risk getting thrown out of a World Series game. To this day people still like to remind me about that play. Jackie was out, he still is.

Maybe I've always been something of a rockhead. I'd always had a few disagreements with Cal Hubbard, a big ump who was a former football player. One time I was catching and he tossed me after missing a third strike. I knew he missed it and I think he knew it, too. So I argued and he told me to get on with the game. I told him I'll play when he admitted he blew one. He said, "Put on your mask," and I said, "I'll put it on when you tell me you missed it," and he threw me out of the game.

Maybe I didn't show proper respect, but that was unusual. I always properly respected the game and my teammates. Sure it got tiring catching doubleheaders

Sometimes we'd get introduced on *The Ed Sullivan Show*, though this probably wasn't one of his really big shows. Ed has his eye on the starlet, and Whitey Ford, me, Moose Skowron, and Mickey Mantle may have a little stage fright.

and playing over 150 games a year. But it was always important for me to be the best teammate I could be—all of us shared that attitude.

Every year I go up to the Hall of Fame in Cooperstown for the inductions. It's a great day, a real happy occasion. You get to see all the guys again and you welcome in another great ballplayer. If I have one minor complaint, sometimes the speeches are too long. Some just wash over you. Not Ryne Sandberg's speech in 2005, though. He did a heck of a job. I remember sitting there thinking everything he said was so true, especially about respecting the game and being a good teammate.

"My managers, like Don Zimmer and Jim Frey, they always said I made things easy on them by showing up on time, never getting into trouble, being ready to play every day, leading by example, being unselfish," Sandberg said. "I made things easy on them? These things they talk about, playing every day, that was my job. I had too much respect for them and for the game to let them down. I was afraid to let them down. I didn't want to let them down or let the fans down or my teammates or my family or myself."

The only way to earn trust is to earn it. If you're on a team, it's up to you to prove yourself. Don't slack off in training. Never give the idea you're not committed—even in practice. Like that saying says, you play like you practice. Not everybody's a great player like Ryne Sandberg. Not everybody can do things great, because they can't. But good team guys, even the most marginal players, always work on their game. They try to do everything as well as they can because that's all you can ask.

Stirring with Reggie

Someone once said you don't have to love Reggie to play alongside him. That's true with any teammate—as long as he's benefiting the team. Reggie gave the Yankees confidence they'd win. . . . In a big situation teammates trusted him.

BEING ON A TEAM, not everyone's going to get along. That's okay. There's differences, because everyone's different. They've got different personalities, come from different backgrounds, have different motivations. When I was a coach for the Yankees in the late 1970s, teammates griped about their own teammates. There was some intense tension in that clubhouse. Most guys weren't thrilled with Reggie Jackson. A lot of that stuff in that ESPN miniseries *The Bronx Is Burning* was real true. Maybe the truest was how Reggie had trouble fitting in.

We'd gotten him as a free agent in 1977 after one season in Baltimore and now he was a Yankee. And the Yankees hadn't won a World Series since '62. So in his first spring training, Reggie said everything on the team would flow through him. He did things nobody else could do. Some thought that meant yapping in front of the media and ticking off his teammates, because he did that awfully darn good. Guys like Thurman Munson, Graig Nettles, and Chris Chambliss prided themselves as Yankees, team guys. They immediately resented Reggie. So did Billy Martin, who dismissively called him "George's boy." Since Reggie was mouthy and craved attention, some guys just wished he'd get lost. "He was him, and we were us," Ron Guidry would say.

Reggie was a Yankee for only five years, but the tradition was important to him. He took being a Yankee real serious. He'd press me and Ellie Howard on where he would've stacked on our championship teams in the '50s. "A fifth outfielder," Ellie told him.

Some of us could joke with him; Billy couldn't. It took all my strength to restrain Billy from slugging Reggie in the dugout in Boston after he pulled him from the game in mid-inning. Those were crazy times. It was the Bronx Zoo, and Reggie was usually front and center.

For all his ego and bluster, everyone came to understand Reggie for what he was. He had this knack for making a good team better. He cared deeply about winning. He had a good work ethic and always felt "relaxedness" in pressure situations like the World Series. He was also a good hustle-type player. After his first few stormy seasons, he gave advice and encouraged the younger players. In 1981 when we got Dave Winfield, Reggie didn't fuss even though Winfield was paid three times more than him. Still, Reggie always wanted to be seen and heard. Some guys wondered if he actually tried as hard in the regular season as in October, when everyone was watching. That I couldn't say, but I do know he gloried in himself. We used to say his goal was to die in his own arms.

Someone once said you don't have to love Reggie to play alongside him. That's true with any teammate— as long as he's benefiting the team. Reggie gave the Yankees confidence they'd win, just like we always had with Whitey Ford, although Whitey kept his self-confidence to himself. Reggie could be a diva and a disruption, but the results are the results; in a big situation teammates trusted him.

People ask how the Yankees won in 1977 and 1978 with all that fighting and fussing. Well, good teams aren't one-man shows. Good teams, like those Yankees, can overcome personality differences. As long as players produce. As long as players can be trusted to be team-oriented. And Reggie did a lot of little things to help win. Those Yankees didn't have the greatest togetherness. But they trusted each other's commitment.

Thirty years later, the Yankees didn't trust a certain teammate's commitment. That's a big problem on any team, anytime. Carl Pavano's off-field problems became problems because the Yankees were counting on him. His teammates were unsure he was doing all he could to pitch and help the team. Mike Mussina got criticized for openly challenging Pavano. If that's what was needed, maybe that's what was needed. Personally I'm not the biggest fan of calling out or embarrassing a teammate. It's usually the coach or the manager's job to tell a player to shape up. John Wooden's biggest rule was not allowing teammates to criticize teammates. When I played for Casey Stengel, he never allowed us to get mad at each other, either; he'd walk around the clubhouse after a losing game to make sure. He was the one who did all the criticizing.

Yet I think there are times a teammate should pull a teammate aside. If he's letting the team down, not trying his hardest, let him know. Remind him the team's counting on him and needs him to be better. And try to make it encouraging. I remember when Eddie Lopat, one of our veteran pitchers, lost patience when Mickey Mantle was a struggling rookie; Eddie was always even-keeled, but not this time. Mickey would get so upset over striking out, he'd sometimes lose concentration in the outfield. Once he didn't get a ball he should've gotten and Lopat really let him have it. He pulled him aside in the dugout the next inning and yelled, "You want to play? If not, get your ass the hell out of here. We don't need guys like you. We want to win."

Basically, Eddie was saying teammates are dependent on each other. We don't need self-absorbed players. Mickey got sent to the minors shortly after and returned later in the season, more confident and with a better attitude. The rest is history.

When a player gets injured off the field or in the off-season, does he owe teammates an apology? That's a hard one. Teammates count on teammates. But teammates also have their own lives. They've got to make their own decisions and take responsibility for themselves. Riding a motorcycle (many players do) and getting seriously injured (some have), you have some answering to do. You hurt yourself. You hurt the team if you can't play or play as well as before.

Two guys on the Yankees lost their lives flying their own planes. I know Thurman Munson and Cory Lidle were both self-assured and independent, both great team guys. And both, I'm sure, had a this-could-never-happen-to-me attitude.

Being young and strong, the risks are easy to ignore. Getting in a motorcycle accident was a painful lesson for guys like Jeff Kent, Kellen Winslow Jr., and Ben Roethlisberger. They issued apologies. But apologies are only words, and now the words that really carry meaning are those in the contract prohibiting danger-ous activities.

We never had those words in our contracts, or I don't remember we did. But our bosses told us we'd better bag any activity that could hurt us.

After my second full season with the Yankees, I worked out a few times with the St. Louis Flyers, the minor-league hockey team back home. It was fun, prac-ticing with those guys. That stopped after they ran a picture of me in the papers. George Weiss, our general manager, immediately called me and told me to get the hell off those skates. I wasn't thrilled. I enjoyed play-ing, and it wasn't a bad way to stay in shape. But I never laced on skates again. Weiss never put a no-hockey clause in my contract, didn't need to. What'd happen if a puck hit me in the eye? he asked. Why screw up my livelihood?

I gave him that, but didn't give in much else contract-wise. We had a few squabbles. Our contracts came up every year, and us players negotiated our-selves. I always based it on my team value and respon-sibilities overall. In 1951, for example, I held out for $40,000. I'd hit .322 the previous year with 124 RBIs, and nobody expected us to win the pennant in '50. Still, Weiss was tough to budge. So I told him I also had to support my mom and dad. I had a wife and a new baby, and there were responsibilities being a Yankee, too. I told him it took dough to dress like a Yankee and act like a Yankee, and the Yankee image was real important to him.

Every team has an image. Ours was supposedly businesslike and efficient; it was always said rooting for the Yankees is like rooting for U.S. Steel, which I guess in the 1950s was pretty businesslike and efficient. Whitey Ford was so businesslike that Ellie Howard called him "Chairman of the Board." The front office was cold and shrewd, kind of like the kind on Wall Street.

The great Green Bay Packers teams of the '60s also had this image of discipline and precision. Vince Lombardi used to compare his team to a large corporation, "like GM, IBM, or Chrysler."

Of this whole corporate thing, we players didn't see it. We weren't uppity or cocky or anything like that. We played good and got along good. Every guy played a role when needed. And we just were in the business of winning. That was serious business. In my rookie year, I doubled my salary just through the winning World Series shares. Sure we had a good top-to-bottom organization—good scouting brings good ballplayers. But we played with terrific skill and spirit. People wondered why we used to beat the Brooklyn Dodgers in the World Series, because they were a heck of a team, too. We had a great rivalry, playing them six times in the Series from 1947 to 1956, winning all but once. We had tremendous respect for those guys—Jackie, Roy Campanella, Duke Snider, Gil Hodges, Pee Wee, Carl Furillo. But we never focused on them. We concentrated on ourselves. We were only concerned about doing what we had to do. All I'd tell our pitchers was to move the ball around, lots of breaking and off-speed stuff in Yankee Stadium, which was bigger than Ebbets Field—even if they hit it four hundred feet, they'd be outs. In Ebbets, keep the pitches down, keep it simple.

Why did we win? We kept it simple and maybe had a little more confidence in each other. Before the 1952 Series, Billy Loes, one of the Dodgers pitchers, actually picked the Yankees to win in seven games. His manager, Charlie Dressen, saw it in the papers and asked Loes if he was crazy, picking against his team. Billy said he made a mistake. "I meant Yankees in six," he said. In those days, we were friends with the Dodgers off the field. On the field we tried like heck to beat each other. The rivalry was fun and intense. The Dodgers played in a bandbox with howling fans. Their team image was a bum. We played in a baseball palace, double the capacity of Ebbets. Our logo was a striped top hat and our fans were accustomed to winning.

Make no mistake, the Yankees were pretty image-conscious. We prided ourselves on being professional. Jackets and ties were required on road trips. Even when Casey took over in 1949, the Yankees were the Yankees. Casey may have humanized us a bit. He loved to double-talk and tell stories to the writers. But he could be gruff in the dugout and ran the games the way he wanted.

We players made sure we ran ourselves, though. Casey knew well enough to let us fix whatever was wrong—all he wanted was aggressive baseball, us thinking about what we were doing at all times. We players had our own meetings and didn't have a captain, didn't need one.

Casey had what he called the honor system. He felt it was up to each player to take care of himself. During the season, we had some guys who liked going out at night. And Casey understood, since he'd spend most of the night at the hotel bar. He'd say, "Just make sure I don't catch any of you mailing letters at four o'clock in the morning."

When he was a player, Casey's manager was John McGraw, a fiery fellow who motivated through fear. Casey motivated through fear and sarcasm. He did a lot of rambling, which was mostly for the writers. But we knew what he meant. He was severe on executing and giving it your all—and expected you to play hurt.

Maybe it was the old ballplayer in him because he didn't mind guys who occasionally raised heck. I like the story during Casey's career when he noticed he and teammate Irish Meusel were being trailed by a detective. He complained to McGraw that he didn't deserve such treatment.

When McGraw asked how he should be treated, Casey said, "I got a right to have a whole detective to myself."

With Casey as manager, we never had a player traded for having too many drinks, or coming in too late. However, one of his favorites, Billy Martin, was traded as a scapegoat.

Everyone called Billy "Casey's boy." He hustled as much as anyone ever hustled. He was scrappy and tough, a heck of a ballplayer. Yet he never was in high favor with George Weiss, the general manager. Weiss just felt he was a bad influence on Mickey, nightlife-wise. That famous fight in the Copacabana in 1957 wasn't Billy's fault—he wasn't even accused of doing anything—but it didn't matter. Weiss traded him to Kansas City right after, and Billy never got over it. "How can you be a bad influence on six pennant winners?" he said. And he never got over that Casey supposedly never stuck up for him. I think Casey did, but lost.

The Copa rhubarb was all over the papers and embarrassing to management. I know Weiss used it as an excuse to get rid of Billy. And as a warning to the rest of us about staying out late.

It all never should've happened. A few of the guys—Hank Bauer, Whitey Ford, Mickey Mantle, and Johnny Kucks—decided to go out with their wives to dinner and celebrate Billy's twenty-ninth birthday. I'd been in a bit of a slump, and Carmen convinced me we should join them and I'd feel better. Billy wasn't married at the time and came alone.

After dinner we all went to see a show at the Copacabana, a real popular nightspot in those days. That's when we got in an argument with some guys heckling Sammy Davis. It ended with Hank Bauer being accused of punching a drunk guy in the bathroom. It was actually one of the Copa bouncers who hit him with a blackjack. Yet the next morning, there was big splashy news about the New York Yankees in a brawl. Each of us there was fined $1,000, except for Kucks, who was the youngest and lowest paid. He got off with $500.

Like I said, the brawl wasn't the fault of anyone. The charges against Hank were all dropped, and the Yankees returned the money to all of us after the season. It's like I told Weiss at the time, "Nobody did nothin' to nobody." Billy just happened to be the victim.

I'm glad I played when I did, no regrets. Sure, there's more prosperity today. More big money in sports, seems everyone's a millionaire or richer. But I can't change a thing, so why would I? Besides, I still cherish the team atmosphere we had. On our teams, nobody dragged anyone down by worrying about their stats or their salary. It didn't matter if you were Joe DiMaggio or Joe De Maestri, the good of the ballclub *always* came first. The relationships with your teammates and how well you played together were more important than anything.

That said, Yankees management didn't always make it easy. Weiss didn't want us to talk to anyone about our salaries. And negotiating with him was usually unpleasant. He didn't give you a thing. He'd find fault in your statistics or value to the team and would always factor potential World Series money into your contract. When Vic Raschi griped about a salary cut in 1954, he got sold to St. Louis to discourage others from complaining about their contracts.

Some of my dealings with George weren't fun, either. After I hit .322 and we won our second straight championship in 1950, I thought $40,000 wasn't unreasonable. Of course, Weiss never thought like I thought and offered $30,000. After a lot of haggling, we settled at $32,000. He was even tougher on Mickey.

When Mickey won the Triple Crown in 1956, he was making $32,500—better than most but not near what the game's best players were making. When Mickey asked for $65,000, Weiss said he couldn't give a guy his age (twenty-five) that kind of increase. And especially to a guy who liked the nightlife. Maybe Weiss spent the extra money on the detectives to trail Mickey.

The golden rule of any team sport is don't put your feelings above the good of the team. Everybody's got to be rowing in the same direction. Of course, not everyone always is. You might have a player disgruntled over playing time or salary. What you don't want is a disgruntled distraction. Even the Yankee teams I played on, we had plenty of grumping over playing time and salaries. But bench players can't let their frustrations or emotions steam over—that can hurt any team's morale.

In youth sports, my feeling is everyone's got to play. When I see kids' games, I see kids being kids. Some are better than the others. Some might not even be very good. That's okay. Let 'em play. What's the purpose of having kids play sports when you don't let them play? It shouldn't be the end of Western civilization if some less skilled twelve-year-old kid messes up in a town soccer game.

Too many kids in youth sports don't see enough action. It's the best way to turn a kid off. And too many adults get too involved, too wrapped up in winning. That makes the games too pressurized, too stressful. I'm not so crazy about the Little League World Series because it's gotten so serious; kids boo-hooing when they lose, to me, is sad.

More than ever, kids don't need screaming adults. They need supportive parents, good coaches, and to be reminded that they won't accomplish things totally on their own. What parent doesn't want his or her kid to succeed? But when it's more important for the parent than the kid, that's a problem. Kids are kids. They need to learn about rules and teamwork. What they don't need is to be embarrassed and criticized. They don't need to hear officials being demeaned. Kids are impressionable about what they see and hear.

Find Your Role

To keep that course, players must adjust to special roles—even roles they don't terribly love. . . . Getting every player to understand his role is important. Even if a player sits next to the watercooler most of the game, he's still part of the club.

A WINNING TRADITION DOESN'T come overnight. It's like what they say in some high schools—you don't graduate tradition. You carry it on. To me that's the great thing about the Yankees—they don't live in the past, but they don't forget it, either. You can't deny the importance of guys who always took that tradition seriously.

Tradition is based on familiarity. For example, Tommy Henrich spent his entire eleven-year career (which was interrupted by World War II) with the Yankees. He was from Ohio and was originally signed by Cleveland. But due to a rules violation he got to play for the team he rooted for as a kid—the Yankees. They were the best and he sure helped keep them that way. When I got to the team in '47, Henrich always reminded the younger guys, "Everybody has to go all out, everybody has to play together, or we won't win."

Every successful team has guys like Henrich— a leader in his own role. He helped the Yankees create a championship identity, having been on seven championship teams himself. Tommy was a guy driven by a shared mission. Everything he did, every motivation he had, was driven by team goals, not individual ones. Phil Rizzuto used to recall how he hit a lead-off triple in the first inning in that final game against Boston in '49. What he never forgot is how Tommy, seeing the second baseman was playing deep, took a half swing to get the run home. Gave himself up for the run—and did it many, many times. Team goals always directed his decision making.

That 1949 team was the first of our record five straight championships. After the '53 season, the Yankees gave twelve players a special plaque. The twelve guys were all members of the five straight championship (1949–1953) teams. These guys weren't necessarily the biggest stars—DiMaggio and Henrich and Mantle and Ford didn't play on each of those teams. But the ones who did shared a special pride. It's why I cherish and still wear the "5" ring the Yankees gave us, signifying the five straight championships. It'd never been done in baseball. And it's why when people ask me questions, I always have a question for them: "Name the twelve guys on the five straight championships." They should be remembered, and here they are: Vic Raschi, Jerry Coleman, Bobby Brown, Hank Bauer, Allie Reynolds, Gene Woodling, Charlie Silvera, Johnny Mize, Eddie Lopat, Joe Collins, Phil Rizzuto, and me.

Not all these guys were big stars. They were starters and bench guys, yet all blended together and believed in each other. Joe Collins was a .256 hitter, Charlie Silvera a backup catcher, and Bobby Brown mostly platooned. They all were team players, leaders in their own roles.

Raschi once told me that we had ninety-six guys who played on the Yankees from 1949 to 1953. So we had pretty good turnover, but we never lost efficiency. Raschi was as consistent and competitive a guy as I ever played with. And I'll tell you, he pitched in pain a lot. One time Casey was talking to a reporter about Raschi and touched his head, his arm, and his heart. "He wins because he pitched from here, here, and here." And Raschi was darn proud he was one of those twelve guys who kept the Yankees on a smooth course.

To keep that course, players must adjust to special roles—even roles they don't terribly love. We had Johnny Mize, a big slugger in the National League, but when we got him in '49, his role changed. He was getting older, so he came off the bench and occasionally started at first for us. It was no picnic for him. And he didn't always get his due. Once he went to talk contract with Weiss, who said, "Well, John, you only played part-time." And Mize said, "Yeah, but I played every time they put my name in the lineup."

Still, Mize had great pride and was a real pro. He analyzed everything and turned himself into the best pinch hitter in the game. Always was giving his teammates tips on what to expect from a certain pitcher. But like I said, he didn't get enough credit for being a great team guy. He'd led the National League four times in home runs, which should've made him an automatic for the Hall of Fame. But maybe because he wasn't a home-run star with the Yankees, the writers didn't vote for him. I know it frustrated him for a long time. Finally, twenty-eight years after he retired, the Veterans Committee elected him. They knew what kind of winner he was, even as a role player.

Who said you can't pitch and think at the same time?
Occasionally I'd help out during batting practice
before they invented batting-practice pitchers.

Getting every player to understand his role is important. Even if a player sits next to the watercooler most of the game, he's still part of the club. Even if he's a scrubeenie who doesn't play, he can contribute. It could be as a pinch hitter or a morale booster, but every reserve can help the team. My backup was Charlie Silvera, a great guy who was always encouraging everybody. He appreciated being part of the team and appreciated collecting seven rings and World Series shares though he scarcely played. "If Yankee Stadium is the House That Ruth Built, then my new home in Millbrae [California] is the house that Yogi built," he'd joke.

Guys like that can ease the pressure, bring everyone together. When I first came up, Johnny Lindell was an extra outfielder, a big guy who played hard when he played and a fun guy when he didn't. He described his signing bonus with the Yankees as a "handshake, a comb, and a bar of Lifebuoy," and his pranks always spirited the team. He liked to scare the bejeezus out of Phil Rizzuto. In those days we left our gloves on the field when we were at-bat, and Johnny would find a way to put a snake or mice in Phil's glove. To see Phil jumping and screeching was always a sight to behold.

Years later, I found out about breaking the tension in 1964 when I was managing the Yankees. We'd just lost four straight to the White Sox and were on the team bus to the airport. That's when Phil Linz started playing "Mary Had a Little Lamb" on his harmonica. I was still in a lousy mood and told him to knock it off. Linz didn't hear me, so supposedly Mickey Mantle told him I wanted him to play it louder, which he did. That's when I swatted it away from him, and the incident became big news. I fined Linz $200, case closed. Linz was a free spirit and a utilityman who once said, "You can't get rich sitting on a bench—but I'm giving it a try." After that harmonica episode we won thirty of our last forty-one games to win the pennant. Some people say the Linz incident ultimately got me fired after the season; I think it helped lighten the mood and got us hot, and I always give him credit.

Funny, when we played St. Louis in the World Series that year, the Cardinals had their own flake to help them. Bob Uecker, their backup catcher, was shagging fly balls with a tuba before game 1 in Sportsman's Park. Though Uecker never played in the Series, which the Cardinals won in seven, Tim McCarver said he was a big factor. "If Bob Uecker had not been on the Cardinals, then it's questionable whether we could have beaten the Yankees," he said. "He kept everything so funny that we never had the chance to think of what a monumental event we were taking part in."

Another fun-loving guy I always remember was Moe Drabowsky. He was a journeyman reliever for the Kansas City A's and Baltimore, and I hit the last home run of my career in 1963 off him. Moe did some funny things, like ordering Chinese food in the bullpen and using hotfoots on his teammates, lighting matches on their shoes while they were wearing them. But Hank Bauer, who managed the O's in 1966, said Moe kept the team loose and was his secret weapon in winning the championship that year. Hank got Moe to start when his starters were exhausted, and Moe did a great job.

Point is, every player on every team is valued. Or hopefully knows he is. It's a big reason the Yankees won four championships from 1996 to 2000. Joe Torre defined roles for his role players, made them feel like they couldn't win without them. Guys like Darryl Strawberry and Tim Raines—both main players on other teams—became superb role players sharing left field.

I remember in 1954 when we picked up Enos Slaughter, who was thirty-eight and a regular star with the Cardinals. He was expecting to play regularly, like always, but Casey told him, "My boy, you play when I tell you to play, and you'll stay up here a long time." So Slaughter, an eventual Hall of Famer, became a platoon player with us and went on to play on three more pennant winners.

Players whose playing time is reduced have to take a hard look. You have to be real about yourself. Where do you fit in? How do you keep a good attitude? How do you still make a difference? Like I said, Hank Bauer and Gene Woodling—both good hard-nosed players—*hated* platooning. Each certainly deserved more at-bats. But together they came around and realized how much this way helped the team. We couldn't have won five straight championships without them as an outfield platoon, and Hank admitted it probably lengthened his career.

Later in my career, I platooned at catcher with Elston Howard. I took it as a positive, too, since we needed Ellie's bat and it saved my knees a little more. When I played left field, it got kind of boring, no hitters or umpires to talk to. But 1961 was one of our greatest years; I was thirty-six and nearing the end but was glad I could still contribute.

A lot of Yankees teams I played on had plenty of grumping over playing time and salaries. Every player is a competitor—who doesn't want to play? I felt bad for

My last active job in baseball was bench coach for the Houston Astros in the late 1980s, a position I supposedly originated with the Yankees.

a guy like Johnny Blanchard, who played so little under Casey—he was behind me and Ellie as a catcher—that he was even thinking of quitting the game. And he was only twenty-seven. Fortunately for him, Ralph Houk took over in '61 and told him he needed him. And Johnny became a valuable guy, doing a little catching, a little outfielding, and a little pinch hitting.

When it comes to valuable, nobody on our Yankees teams was more valuable and versatile than Gil McDougald. He'd never played third base in his life when he came up in 1951. When Casey asked him to play it in spring training, Gil said, "They can't do no more than knock my teeth out." Yet he became an All-Star there, just like he became an All-Star at short and an All-Star at second. Usually versatility is a curse. You don't get enough time to settle in and excel at one position. Yet Gil perfected three infield positions and never got the real credit he deserved. He was such a team guy; his defense and clutch hitting were no small reasons we won throughout the '50s. He was always willing and gutsy enough to change positions whenever needed, and what more could you ask for in a player?

Hard to Change

Sometimes to win, players need to change roles.

OF COURSE, IT'S NOT always that simple. Even with guys who are great team players, which Graig Nettles was. At thirty-nine, he was nearing the end when I took over as Yankees manager the second time in 1984. And we'd just gotten Toby Harrah in a trade. The plan was for them to platoon at third. Harrah was a good righty power bat, a proven veteran himself. But Graig told me he still expected to play all the time. He was the team captain and unhappy with the plan. If you're a manager, you don't want an unhappy player, especially an unhappy team captain who's late reporting to training camp.

I always liked what Graig gave the Yankees. He probably never got the credit he deserved. He was a big part of our back-to-back championships in the 1970s, taking in all the Reggie-Billy-George craziness. He had a smart-aleck sense of humor, too. He had that famous line, "When I was a little boy, I wanted to be a baseball player and join the circus. With the Yankees, I've accomplished both." And when Steinbrenner was always erupting, Nettles said, "The more we lose, the more he'll fly in. And the more he flies in, the best the chance there'll be a plane crash." Fittingly, his memoir was called *Balls*.

I was a coach most of Nettles's career with the Yankees. We used to talk about team loyalty a lot; he told me he envied me since baseball wasn't so transient in my day. Guys stayed on one team longer. They were loyal to a tradition. After all Graig had been through—he spent eleven seasons with the Yankees—I think he felt the team should've let him finish his career on his terms. Show him the loyalty. But the Yankees showed him the door. They didn't want a disgruntled player and traded him to San Diego, his hometown. To this day, Graig always jokes that I'm the reason he got traded from the Yankees. Nope, I tell him—he traded himself.

Being a navy man, I liked following David Robinson in basketball. He was the big guy for the San Antonio Spurs in the 1990s, everything went through him. He was their number one star, but not one of those it's-all-about-me stars. They said when the Spurs came off the bus, the girls ran to his teammates and the mothers ran to Robinson.

He won everything you could win—Rookie of the Year, league MVP, Defensive Player of the Year, scoring champ, rebounding champ. But he'd never won a championship in ten years. Then the Spurs got Tim Duncan. So Robinson stepped back without being asked, concentrated more on setting up his teammates, rebounding, team defense, and the team won the 1999 NBA championship. Duncan respected Robinson so much that he stayed in San Antonio although he could've gotten richer elsewhere. A few years later, with Duncan and Tony Parker as the go-to guys, Robinson was thirty-seven with a bad back and playing his farewell season. But even in a lesser role, he was still a difference maker and San Antonio won another title.

Sometimes to win, players need to change roles. Even star players like David Robinson. You see it in basketball a lot. Stars may have to sacrifice salary, playing time, and ego. If you think it's easy, ask someone who's done it—like Bob McAdoo. He was a big star at North Carolina and a three-time NBA scoring champ before joining the Los Angeles Lakers in 1981. Already there were Magic Johnson and Kareem Abdul-Jabbar, so McAdoo wasn't the main guy anymore. He had a lesser role. "It was something I never came to grips with," he told *USA Today*. "I did it for the sake of winning a championship, but it was hard for me mentally and physically to do it in the beginning stages.

"You've been doing something one way for 10 years, starting, playing 40–42 minutes a game, so it was just mind-boggling. . . . I don't care what anybody says—it's hard to deal with."

Sure it's hard. On any team in any sport, any player wants a comfort zone, his best position to succeed. Even Babe Ruth complained about alternating as an outfielder and a pitcher for the Red Sox in 1919, even though he was excellent at both. "I don't think I can keep on playing the outfield when I'm not pitching," he said. "It tires me out too much." When the Yankees got Babe, they told him to forget pitching.

Nobody will ever say DiMaggio wasn't one of the best team players ever. And nobody resented him when he didn't shift to another position easily. That was at the end of his career, when his legs were going and Casey asked him to play first base. Joe wasn't real thrilled. He had too much pride to embarrass himself or his team. "He's worried all over," said Henrich, who was Joe's teammate all those years. "He's afraid of making a dumb play because he's not familiar with first base. It would have killed him to make a stupid play." The experiment didn't work, just like it didn't work for Mike Piazza, who was also asked to play first late in his career.

When you tell a player to change position, you better sell him. Convince him it's not only best for him, it's really best for the team. Show him appreciation and respect, he'll give you his best back. I don't think DiMaggio or Piazza were convinced their shifts were for anyone's betterment. A long time ago, I wasn't convinced Casey Stengel's brainstorm of shifting me to first base was good for anyone.

Of course I took great pride in catching. I worked hard at it. It's where I could do my most good. But in the late 1950s, we had Elston Howard, whose best position was catcher, too. I would play more and more in the outfield as Ellie played more behind the plate. Not a big deal. I played there in my early years. Plus, I knew I could help the team in the outfield. At the end of my career, I even got put in left field in late innings for defense.

But in 1959, Casey was pushing this idea of making me try first base, too. I had played it as a kid, but I didn't go for it and let Casey know it. I didn't care that there weren't any squat five-foot-eight first basemen around. Honestly, I cared more how this would affect the Yankees. It was already going to be a terrible season for us. Always I prided myself being a team-first guy, but in this case I might've been a teammate-first guy. We had Moose Skowron at first, and the last thing he needed was me taking his job. Guys already ribbed Moose a lot. Once he got hurt, and Kent Hadley, a throw-in in the Roger Maris trade, hit two homers his first two times up. Everyone started calling Moose "Wally Pipp," the first baseman who let Gehrig take his place.

I felt that me playing first was unnecessary because I could help more as a catcher or an outfielder. That's what I told Casey, and he finally gave up but not before jabbing me. One day he came in the clubhouse and said for everyone to hear, "You know why he don't want to play first? He's afraid of the dirty look Skowron will give him if he picks up a first baseman's mitt."

Asking a player to do something he's not used to is hard. One of the hardest things I ever did as a manager was convince Dave Righetti to become a reliever. It was actually a group decision after the 1983 season. Rags had been a starter since he joined the Yankees in 1981 and was Rookie of the Year. And in '83, he pitched a no-hitter against the Red Sox on the Fourth of July— the first by a Yankee since Larsen's perfect game.

Rags came to the Yankees from Texas in the Sparky Lyle trade. People always wondered if his arm would last, he was such a hard thrower, a strikeout pitcher who once struck out twenty-one guys in a minor-league game. He progressed good with the Yankees and seemed on track to succeed Ron Guidry as the number one starter. But then Goose Gossage left the Yankees as a free agent after the '83 season. We suddenly needed a closer. Sammy Ellis, our pitching coach, and I felt Rags could be a good one. And we felt if we used him right, we'd extend his career.

Of course Rags needed serious convincing. He was pretty ticked when we told him the plan. The last thing you want on a team is a guy with a raging attitude. But Rags, to his credit, came around. I promised him I'd never overuse him, that he'd be still strong at season's end. And mostly he was helping the team where we needed help.

Rags was intense, a fierce competitor, and he also had a good wit about him, which is good for a reliever. Those were the days we had Ed Whitson, who had a lot of trouble pitching in New York. He seemed out of sorts when the fans would do that mocking chant, "Ed-die . . . Ed-die." Rags used to tell him not to worry, all the beer vendors at Yankee Stadium were named Eddie.

Main thing is, Rags became a heck of a closer. The year after I was fired (1986) he set a then record for saves with forty-six. A couple of years later he became a free agent, with teams promising to return him as a starter. But Rags re-signed with the Yankees, as a reliever. And he lasted fifteen years pitching in the majors. To this day, he'll still kid me, "Yogi, you never should've changed me."

I'll remind him, look what he started. If not for him, maybe the A's don't change Dennis Eckersley into a closer, and now a Hall of Famer. Maybe the Braves don't do the same with John Smoltz. Those guys could pitch, but they took a risky experiment. They changed their careers for the team good.

Making Everyone Better

How do good teams become even better? A team's best player can have a serious impact . . . by providing confidence, being unselfish, and finding joy in the success of his teammates.

HOW DO GOOD TEAMS become even better? When a team's best player can have a serious impact on his teammates. Mostly it's by providing confidence, being unselfish, and finding joy in the success of his teammates. That's what Steve Nash does so good in Phoenix. It's what Magic Johnson, Larry Bird, and Michael Jordan did so great when they played. It's what also separated Wayne Gretzky, Mario Lemieux, and Steve Yzerman in hockey. They got things done through others—the impact of their actions had a positive effect on others.

Great team players take off the pressure. In 1961, a big reason we all did so great was Mantle and Maris. We won 109 games. Everyone was real relaxed because all the attention was on their home-run hitting and chasing Babe Ruth's record. That year six guys hit over twenty homers, including all three catchers—me, Ellie Howard, and

John Blanchard. And Ellie also hit .348. Whitey won twenty-five games.

Sure, the pressure overwhelmed Roger. He wasn't real talkative with the press, more of a yes-or-no guy. It was a lot of hoopla all year and he never wanted it. Winning the pennant mattered most to him, and just being one of the guys. I remember one game in September, he came up in the first inning with Tony Kubek on third and one out. He bunted for a hit and Kubek scored. In his very next at-bat, he hit his fifty-fifth homer. All the writers asked him afterward, "Why bunt?" And Roger just said, "Why not? They were playing deep and I knew I could get Tony in. We still have a pennant to win."

That was Roger. He was a heck of an all-around player and would do anything for the team. When I was manager in 1964, I told him we needed him in center when Mickey was hurt. No big deal, he just did it. He did everything—run, field, hit, throw, and play a great center field. When Roger was later traded to the Cardinals, I know all those guys loved him as a teammate.

What I learned on the Yankees is that success is learned, practiced, and shared with everyone. It's the same on almost every championship team—then and today. Florida winning back-to-back NCAA basketball titles in 2006 and 2007 was a great example of unselfish play and teamwork. Back in the old days, the Boston Celtics kind of patented those concepts.

Bill Russell sacrificed scoring on the Celtics, because he knew defense wins championships. "To me, one of the most beautiful things to see is a group of men coordinating their efforts toward a common goal, alternately subordinating and asserting themselves to achieve real teamwork in action," he wrote. "I tried to do that, we all tried to do that, on the Celtics. I think we succeeded."

Russell's rebounding, shot-blocking, and defense gave his teammates that extra confidence. It also gave them a killer fast break, a big part of their offense. Because of Russell's team-first attitude his Celtics won a record eleven championships. Russell not only knew his job, he knew it about 500 percent better than most.

When you think of Bill Russell, you're thinking history because he's in the past. Defense and unselfishness aren't real glamorous today. Flashy scorers are more marketable. They sell more jerseys. Not many years ago Red Auerbach, who drafted Russell and coached all those championship teams, walked onto the court at Celtics practice. He heard the players kidding around about who had the best moves, who had the best shot, who was the biggest star. Red waved at them dismissively. "If No. 6 were here," he said, "all you sorry bastards would be shaking in your shoes."

Sometimes you wonder if that attitude is old-fashioned. Or if Russell's intelligence went out of style, too. Things get a little silly with so much hype on individuals in team sports. Why does somebody have to be the Man? Or the Franchise? (When I was coaching the Mets in the late '60s, the owner, M. Donald Grant, used to hate when they called Tom Seaver "the Franchise." "I'm the goddamn franchise," he'd insist.)

Why can't it be Lakers vs. Heat instead of Kobe vs. Shaq? In soccer it was Zidane vs. Ronaldo, but it should've been France vs. Brazil. When the Yankees used to play the Dodgers in the World Series, I guarantee you it was never advertised as Yogi vs. Campy.

Me and Roy Campanella were rivals but also friends. We each won three Most Valuable Player awards, which was nice. But I know he'd agree that no trophy, no records, no amount of money ever equaled the feeling of being part of a championship team. Two of my MVPs came in 1954 and 1955—one year when the Yankees didn't make the World Series and the other when we lost it. I don't blame myself, but maybe I could've been a more valuable player than the most valuable.

Of course, Michael Jordan never won anything in the NBA except individual honors until he really started trusting his teammates. He always made memorable game-winning shots. Yet what always stands out is the 1997 finals when he took a play designed for him and set up Steve Kerr for the series-winning shot. Jordan was hard on his teammates. But he learned he wasn't going to win without them. I think he felt his job was to be the best and his teammates would follow.

Quiet Leaders

Anyone can use a good
mentor, a person who cares
and knows more than you
know.

AFTER I RETIRED as a Houston coach in 1989, I started going to Astros spring training to help out. They had a baby catcher who I actually had seen at Seton Hall, and you knew he was pretty good. I always identified with short catchers—they don't have to stand up as far—and I always liked Pudge Rodriguez because he was short and a good player. Craig Biggio was a little guy, too. You could see Beege was also a special kid, a good player with good ability and the right attitude. When he first came up, Jose Cruz thought Biggio was the batboy and asked him to get a cup of coffee. Biggio told him he was no batboy, but it was nice to meet him, and still offered Cruz a cup of coffee.

All these years Beege stayed humble, respectful. Never was an "I" guy, always a team guy, and he learned it right from those early days. One of the first guys on the Astros to talk to him was Alan Ashby. He was a veteran, the regular catcher, and told Beege he didn't want to lose his job. But Ashby told him he'd help him any way he could, if he ever wanted. Don't think a young guy like Beege didn't appreciate that—he never forgot.

Back then nobody minded if Biggio didn't remind anyone of Johnny Bench—nobody reminds nobody of Johnny anyway. Beege was smallish with a not-great arm. But he worked his tail off making himself an All-Star catcher in just one year.

Then I, for one, helped change his whole career. I wasn't so positive that catcher was best for him long-term or short-term. I thought it'd wear down his legs, and his speed was a good weapon. We coaches talked it over. We told Beege he and the team might be better off if he moved to second base. He was only twenty-six; he could learn fast enough. Next year he played all 162 games and became an All-Star at second. You'd think management would appreciate a team-first guy like Beege and they did. But the Astros made a wrong mistake a few years later when they signed Jeff Kent to play second. And never told Beege he was moving to the outfield. The big lesson? Don't make a change that way. If someone's important, show some respect. It's kind of like when I got fired as Yankee manager in 1985. Being a manager is important and being a Yankee was always important to me. So I felt George Steinbrenner should've told me himself I was gone—I found out through someone else and didn't take it so good. I stayed away fourteen years, a long time, but like I said, I didn't take it so good.

In his case, Beege asked to see the owner, Drayton McLane. He told him he'd shift to the outfield for the team's good. But he also said he didn't want to be judged on how he did at a new position in the last year of his contract. Then Beege worked his tail off to be a good outfielder, even increasing his arm strength. And he even got a contract extension.

I can't say enough about Beege and Jeff Bagwell, who I also got to work with early on. Bags came to the Astros as a kid third baseman in 1991, but Ken Caminiti was established there. I thought he might be good at first base, and Art Howe, the manager, and Bob Watson in the front office agreed. So Art gave Bags a choice—play third in Triple A or first in the majors. Bags never thought twice. He turned himself into one heck of a first baseman and hitter, maybe the best the Astros ever had.

Beege and Bags were like ham and eggs. All those years in Houston, they were perfect together. Both cared about the organization and their teammates. When a tornado destroyed utilityman Tim Bogar's house in Florida, Beege had Bogar's family move in with his. Near the end of Bags's career, he had that bad shoulder and couldn't even play in spring training, but he stayed around the team and helped some of the young hitters, passing along what he knew. Both just did things right, played the game right, like they were old-fashioned. Years ago Beege turned down crazy money to stay in Houston and then switched positions in midseason. If they seem like rarities, they were, because nobody hardly finishes their careers with one team. Old-school guys, like they had in the old days.

Another guy I go back to the beginning with is Don Mattingly. He was another not-so-big player with good ability and fierce competitiveness. He got better and better because he worked and worked and was brutal on himself. Like a perfectionist. He reminded me a little of Mickey Mantle that way. Holy moly, did he take batting practice—he used to go in the cage ninety minutes a day every day—and that'd be in the off-season. He was kind of intense about it, and I used to tell him, "Don, you're going to hit yourself right into a slump."

I first saw Mattingly in Nashville in 1981, the year of the strike. I was a Yankee coach, and George Steinbrenner sent me around to see the farm system. Truth is the Yankees were already talking of getting rid of him—he was only twenty—because he didn't pull the ball, and they didn't know where he'd play. But you could see he was a hitter. He didn't strike out. I knew he'd be okay.

"Leave him alone." That was my report to George's baseball people. Unfortunately they should've also left alone the skinny centerfielder on that team—Willie McGee. The Yankees wrongly gave up on a lot of young guys in those days. They also went the whole 1980s with no World Series.

When I became manager in '84, I told Donnie he was my regular first baseman, don't worry about being yo-yoed. So he hit .343 and won the batting title, the youngest Yankee to do so since Mickey in 1956. When a reporter asked me if he exceeded expectations, I said he'd done more than that.

I got fired early the next season, but I always followed Donnie, and we'd chat over the winter. He just had that professionalism. He just went about his business, and every teammate respected the heck out of him.

One year the Yankees didn't have a third baseman because of injuries. So Donnie volunteered to play there, even though he's left-handed. Now, left-handed third basemen are practically unheard of because there are none, because a lefty third baseman has to twist his body to throw across the infield and make awkward throws on double-play balls. But Donnie did it for a few games, anyway. Didn't care about getting embarrassed or injured. He did it because the team needed someone.

It's a shame Donnie's career ended too soon. His back got too bad, and he really wasn't the same player. But he was the same person, honest and true. And his teammates respected him so much that they wanted to get to the playoffs awfully bad in 1995. They knew this was Donnie's last chance. When the Yankees signed Darryl Strawberry for the stretch run that year, there was grumbling in the clubhouse. Strawberry had a history of problems. He'd been kicked out of baseball for drug use and was known to be a distraction. So Donnie did what an honest team man does—support his teammate. "I wanted Darryl to know that I did not care what had happened in the past, that as long as he was ready to play ball, he was welcome in my clubhouse. I knew exactly what I was doing, what I was saying. I knew that if I was on Darryl's side, it would be easier for him to make it in the Bronx."

Strawberry did, becoming a valuable part-time player at the end of his career.

It was also the end of Mattingly's career. I think his popularity resembles Jeter's, who succeeded him as captain. What Donnie did was give everyone—the fans, his teammates—all of him every time he was on the field.

Nobody outworked him and he never made excuses. He stayed out of trouble and played the game right. And he could hit, too.

Talking about guys who knew how to hit and lead by example, let me talk about Stan Musial. He was the Man before it became the big slogan that you see everywhere. He was Stan the Man all right, but his friends called him Stash. For all of Musial's accomplishments—he won seven batting titles—he was an even better person. Every teammate during Stash's twenty-two years on the Cardinals loved him. The thing about him was he was always easygoing, relaxed. He said why get upset that he went 0-for-4? He knew he'd get three hits the next day.

We'd see him in spring training at the pool halls in St. Petersburg, just one of the guys, always a smile on his face. He had friendships with everyone. I got to know him in spring training (we shared the same spring base as the Cardinals) and back home in St. Louis. We'd play golf a couple times a week at the Sunset Country Club. He meshed with fans and teammates and became partners with Biggie Garagnini, who owned a restaurant on Chippewa Avenue. That's the place where I first met Carmen, who was working as a waitress. She thought I was unusual because I'd come in wearing my golf shoes. She knew about Stan Musial but didn't know anything about me—I'd just finished my rookie year with the Yankees.

Some guys were in awe of Stash because he was a tremendous player, but he was always funny and modest. Just a little ol' singles hitter, he called himself. Yeah, right. He had great confidence, and that's what

Carmen, my bride of fifty-nine years and still a real beauty. Everyone should have a boss like her.

impressed everyone, though he never had to impress anyone. How confident was he? All-Star Games in those days were serious business. Players wanted to win bad. In the 1955 All-Star Game in Milwaukee, it was the twelfth inning and getting dark. We'd been out there almost three and a half hours, and Stash is the oldest player in the game and tells me he's getting weary. I tell him my feet are tired, too. And ain't it a shame nobody can see the ball through the shadows? Stash tells me to relax, says we're all going home soon. And he smashed the first pitch for a home run.

The joy he had playing ball was contagious. Stash made everyone around him feel better. Once a journeyman infielder on the Cardinals named Tom Glaviano told him, "I prayed for you last night. Got down on my knees and prayed." Stash said he didn't realize Glaviano thought that much of him. "Don't get me wrong," Glaviano said. "I was thinking what I could do with all that World Series dough."

Actually Stash won three World Series (1942, 1944, 1946). But he always regretted that the Cardinals could never catch the Dodgers or the Giants in the '50s. He knew it was because they were one of the last teams to integrate.

When the Cards did bring in black players, Curt Flood was the first to be a regular in 1958. A year later they got Bill White, who like Stash also played first base. "Stan was helpful to anyone who asked him for advice," said White. "It didn't make any difference to him who you were." Soon enough, Stash would shift to left field to make room for White, who became one of the best first basemen in the league. In 1962, Musial, at forty-one years old, hit .330 as an outfielder.

He never forgot the people who helped him. Mostly Dickie Kerr, his mentor. If you're lucky to have a mentor, you're fortunate. I had one with Bill Dickey and never forgot the lesson of passing along my experience. Phil Rizzuto was like a mentor to me, too. He was a few years older, became my roommate, and used to tell me things I should know about life in the majors. He convinced me to move to New Jersey, and we worked together in the off-season, even opening up our own bowling alley. Phil's the godfather to my oldest son, Larry.

Willie Mays was twenty when he was mentored by Monte Irvin, one of the greatest guys I know. Willie was kind of shy and scared back then, but Monte roomed with him and kept boosting his confidence. Years later, after Willie became a big star, he took Bobby Bonds under his wing. In 1969, only his second season in the majors, Bobby became the first guy ever to hit thirty homers and steal thirty bases in one season.

Anyone can use a good mentor, a person who cares and knows more than you know. Musial was always indebted to Kerr, a former big-league pitcher who managed him in the minors when Stash was a nineteen-year-old left-handed pitcher. One day Stash fell on his left shoulder and his arm just went dead. Kerr never gave up on him. He befriended him, kept pep-talking him, convinced him to become a hitter. He convinced Musial his arm would improve so he could play the outfield. Which he did. Stash eventually won batting titles playing three positions—left field, center field, and first base. He always said it wouldn't have happened if not for Kerr. Stash even named his son after him, and years later, when Kerr and his wife were going through hard times, Stash bought him a nice house in Texas.

Who doesn't appreciate being appreciated? One of the best things in sports is the little gesture to acknowledge an unselfish play. In basketball, Bobby Jones is credited for starting it; he's the former NBA player who used to point to the guy whose pass set him up for a basket. Jones actually started doing it in college at North Carolina, where his coach, Dean Smith, ordered his players to point in appreciation for a teammate's teamwork.

Here's my two cents on appreciation. When you're appreciated you can do some terrific things. My old buddy Larry Doby was the first black to play in the American League. When he joined the Indians in July 1947, the manager, Lou Boudreau, introduced him to his teammates. Ten guys refused to shake his hand. The next year most of those guys were gone and the Indians won the World Series. Still, there was a lot of prejudice in those days. I know Larry was quiet, emotionally sensitive. He kept his troubles inside. I'd chat with him at the plate, just like any opposing hitter, and we eventually became friends.

I know he always appreciated that famous newspaper picture of him and white pitcher Steve Gromek hugging in the clubhouse in the '48 Series. It showed people that he was appreciated by his teammates. Larry used to say the big difference between a good ballplayer and a great one is confidence. And he once told me it wasn't until 1954 when he felt the most confidence, the most relaxed in his mind. Mostly because there was a different feeling on Cleveland that year. His teammates were more unified. In those days black players like Doby were brushed back a lot.

But Early Wynn and the other pitchers would protect them by knocking down the opposing hitters. That '54 Indians team was the most together Indians team I remember. One game, Larry leaped over the left-center barrier in Cleveland and fell hard in snagging a sure home run. The pitcher, Art Houtteman, waited on the mound for Larry to run in to thank him for what Dizzy Dean, who announced the game on radio, called "the greatest catch I've seen in my life."

That season, Larry didn't make an error in center field and led the league in RBIs with 126, and the Indians won a record 111 games. They beat us by eight games; their togetherness helped everyone play at a very high level. "You know," Larry told one of the Cleveland writers, "I feel like I'm in my rookie year—like I'm just starting my baseball career—that I've wasted a lot of time up 'til now."

Respect Your Team

It's the players who invest in their team-first attitude. They're the ones who charge fines to a teammate if he's late to a team meeting or screws up in practice. Good teams keep themselves in line.

GROWING UP, I LEARNED about respect. I respected my pop telling me I'd better respect whatever he said. Pop wasn't old school. He was Old World. He came over from Italy before World War I, trying to support his family in a new land. He was a laborer in the brickyards, as was Joe Garagiola's dad. Pop knew little English, but he knew hard work. He also made sure we knew the language of respect.

None of us five kids ever left the dinner table until he got up first. If I went out at night and promised Pop I'd be home at a certain time, I'd darn not be a minute late. And if I didn't have his tureen of beer waiting for him after the four-thirty whistle blew at the Laclede-Christy brickworks, trouble awaited me.

If I learned anything being Pietro Berra's son, it was punctuality and respect. They became lifelong habits. Getting to an appointment early. Being one of the first to get to the ballpark. To this day, I still get up early, always at 6 A.M., no matter what time I went to bed the night before. Being punctual for work or getting early to team practice, I think it shows something. In sports it shows you care. It tells your teammates what you think of them.

When you show up late, it gives a different impression. It's the idea that you play by your own rules. That's why coaches and managers always have a bug about being on time. About discipline and team commitment. It could be a pregame stretch or a team meeting or a curfew. If you're late, you pay. Them's the rules, as we'd say. Unless you have an excuse, there's no excuse—every player has a contract to follow team rules.

On the Yankees, though, we mostly policed ourselves. When Casey took over as Yankee manager in 1949, he didn't have a whole lot of rules. We just had guys like Hank Bauer, who'd let you know if you were messing up. He let Whitey Ford know it as soon as he came up to the bigs in mid-July 1950. Whitey happened to oversleep before his first major-league start. He got to the stadium clubhouse later than everyone, but fortunately did okay enough to win the game. Afterward, Bauer went up to him at his locker and told him, honest to heaven, if he'd lost, he'd be dead. Whitey went on to win nine of ten games and helped us win the pennant.

It's no big surprise that the New England Patriots enforce themselves, too. It's the players who invest in their team-first attitude. They're the ones who charge fines to a teammate if he's late to a team meeting or screws up in practice. Good teams keep themselves in line.

That's not always easy. Sometimes I think more players care more about other things. They don't always care about anyone else. That carries over into after-hours carousing and off-field troubles. They stray from the rules. Including the ones that govern their team.

We always tell the kids at our museum how Alexander J. Cartwright, who started the first organized baseball club in 1845, wrote a set of twenty rules. One of those rules included punctuality for players. At least it's good in theory.

Babe Ruth wasn't always good on punctuality. One time in 1925 Ruth stayed out all night. He came into the Yankee locker room the next day, too late to take batting practice. Miller Huggins, the manager, was furious and told Ruth not to bother dressing. He suspended him and fined him $5,000—an awful lot in those days, actually 10 percent of Ruth's salary. Ruth appealed the punishment to the Yankees owner, Colonel Jacob Ruppert, but no dice. Which goes to show that the team is always bigger than one player, even if the player happens to be the greatest ever.

Being on time is about self-discipline. I never saw more self-discipline than in Japan, where I've visited three times—as a Yankees player in 1955, as a Mets manager in 1974, and as part of the Yankees contingent in 2004. Much has changed in Japan over the years. Obsession with punctuality hasn't. Last time we visited, someone told us that a Japanese farmer killed his brother because he was late to work. When they say, "Don't be late," they're not fooling around. Mostly, if you're late, you're rude, disrespectful. And respect is a big, big, big thing over there.

Like I said, it's forever been a big thing with me, too. If people value my time, I value theirs. When I was one of the first to arrive at Yankee Stadium before a game, Casey used to joke it was my excuse to get out of the house. To me, I just got out of the house earlier than the others.

People who know me know I'm known for punctuality. Maybe you remember I stayed away from Yankee Stadium for a long time. That's when I was fired by George Steinbrenner and didn't like how he did it. So after fourteen years, George decided to make his peace with me. He flew up from Tampa to our museum in New Jersey. When he finally arrived a few minutes after he was scheduled, I was standing there waiting for him. I looked at my watch and said, "You're late." George appreciated the jab, since he used to be the King of Impatience.

Sometimes baseball isn't like other team sports. There's so much closeness. The clubhouse is the players' other house. Players spend more time with their teammates than with their families. There's a lot of foolishness that goes on. When someone does something silly on or off the field, it's easy for a teammate to shrug it off, "That's Manny being Manny."

If you can count on a teammate, you can forgive a lot of transgressions. That said, there will always be teammate conflicts. Some people are difficult, some aren't, everyone's different. There will never be a locker room of twenty-five best friends. That's how it is. I've seen teammates who never said hello to each other. I've seen teammates in crazy turmoil, like the Yankees in the late 1970s.

Clubhouse tension isn't the ideal recipe for success. But if you don't like someone in your own locker room, you sure as heck better get along on the field. The Oakland A's were always fussing and feuding in the early 1970s. Bill North and Reggie Jackson especially irritated each other. But once the game started, everyone's focus was on one single thing—winning. The A's disliked each other but won three straight championships, because as North said, "You don't have to love a guy to play ball alongside him."

If you can't separate personal from professional, somebody's got to go. When you see pitchers and catchers tussling in the dugout, that's bad. It's distracting. It affects the team—not a winning situation.

All my playing years with the Yankees, the closest thing to a fight we had was in 1958. We'd just clinched the pennant and were on a train to Detroit. Ryne Duren, our big relief pitcher, had probably had too much to drink. For some reason, he went up to Ralph Houk, then our first-base coach, and told him he had always wanted to push his cigar down his throat, and they got into a scuffle. But it had no negative consequence to the team. Nobody told the press about it. Duren and Houk patched things up and we went on to win the World Series.

I grew up rooting for the St. Louis Cardinals in the 1930s—the Gashouse Gang. Dizzy Dean, Rip Collins, Pepper Martin, Ducky Medwick—those guys could play. They could also fight. Even with each other. Despite all their scrapping, their desire to be the best never cooled. My favorite player on those teams was Medwick, who was a great hitter with a real short-fuse temper.

Some guys just play good mad, and it wasn't unusual for Medwick to act like a madman or threaten his teammates. Once he bopped his own pitcher, Tex Carleton, for taking too many swings in batting practice.

On some Saturdays, a bunch of us went to Sportsman's Park and sat in the left-field stands, where I watched Medwick. He became my idol because I liked his unusualness of swinging at bad balls. I kind of adopted his philosophy myself—if I could see it, I figured I could hit it. Bill Dickey told me of a time in the 1934 All-Star Game when Medwick jumped and hit a homer on a pitch so high that Dickey said he probably couldn't have caught it.

Whatever they say about Joe Medwick being abrasive, I saw the opposite. When I was ten or eleven selling newspapers on the corner of Southwest and Kingshighway, he was my customer. Medwick would gave me a nickel for a three-cent paper—pretty good back then—and chat for a few minutes before driving off. Little did I know my idol would become a good pal.

By 1947, Medwick's greatness was gone. He came to spring training with the Yankees that season trying to hang on. I was a rookie, nervous since I had no guarantee, either. But Medwick gave me a few tips on playing the outfield, and that's where I started my first season in the bigs. A month later, Joe got released from the club. After that season, he called and invited me to play golf at Sunset Golf Club back in St. Louis, and I got fixated on the game. He also came to my wedding. Years later he came to my induction to the Hall of Fame. I never apologize for saying Joe Medwick was my idol.

Medwick was a great ballplayer and a great RBI man, and he won the Triple Crown in 1937. True, he never won Mr. Congeniality. His hard slide in the '34 World Series prompted a near-riot in Detroit. And some of his teammates really couldn't stand him. Many believe he was purposely beaned in the temple by his former Cardinals teammate Bob Bowman. Whatever, he really wasn't the same player afterward.

Supposedly his grumpiness kept him out of election into the Hall for years, or so it was rumored. Johnny Mize, a teammate of Medwick on the Cardinals, said Joe usually wasn't happy unless he was snarling at somebody. But he said he was the true guts of the Gashouse Gang. Nobody cared more about winning.

Those Cardinals teams with Dizzy Dean and Joe Medwick were characters. They raised a rumpus and played the game rough-and-tumble. Whether they bragged or jawboned or slugged anyone around them, they never let down the guys wearing the same uniform. For all his own achievements, Medwick truly cared most about the team as a whole. Whenever I think of the Gashouse Gang, I don't think of dissension. If you lose, it's dissension. When you win, it's spirit.

Not Over Till It's Over

On a team, the most important thing isn't the accomplishments. It's the relationships. Being on a team isn't just being a member; it's giving of yourself for the team good. It's collaborating, sacrificing, trusting, and working together. Working together works.

BUSINESS AND SPORTS ARE similar today. People are people and they're supposed to produce. Still, organizations push for immediate results or a quick turnaround. You don't see too much long-term strategy or patience. There's more college and pro coaches changing jobs than ever. Teams want and expect to win—now. It just makes everyone more impatient.

Usually some crisis in an organization causes change. I think that's what happened when I got fired in 1964, after my first year as Yankee manager. Supposedly management made their decision in August, when we were struggling and me and Phil Linz had that harmonica incident. I was let go two days after the World Series.

That year I was learning on the job. When I got to the Mets, I learned about changing the team culture. We were lovable losers. Then Gil Hodges came to the Mets. He brought professionalism and accountability. He'd already managed in Washington, so he had some experience. Gil was great to me. I was already on the coaching staff and he could've brought his own man. But he knew that I knew the game and asked me to help. He put a lot of trust in his coaches. People thought we were enemies from the Yankee-Dodger rivalry, but we weren't. We got along great. Gil inspired respect from every player, and his no-nonsense style rubbed off on every player. We surprised the whole country in 1969 because Gil kept preaching the basics—discipline, fundamentals, team play.

When people ask me what really makes a good manager, that's easy. Good players. Casey Stengel was no different. He was a managerial loser before coming to the Yankees in 1949. But given players who could play and execute, he won. Preaching team play made him a big winner.

Same with Joe Torre and Bill Belichick, both failures on other teams, too. But they got better players, used patience and intelligence, and got their players to believe in their method. Joe did a great job with the Yankees for more than a decade, and Belichick made a great dynasty out of the Patriots. They never let pressure affect them; they're calm and firm and foster an attitude for players to give of themselves for the good of the team.

Team and trust go together. Trust is a great motivator. It brings out the best in people. But you can't assume that trust develops naturally as part of the team's personality. If you're a manager or a coach, you have to get each team member to understand what it means, how it works, and why it matters. You could tell that Willie Randolph has built trust on the Mets, and Eric Mangini on the Jets. Like their old bosses Torre and Belichick, they are smooth and disciplined. They're both serious and patient, but don't try their patience. They're more old school than their mentors.

I think it's easy to overlook the value of patience. Especially these days when lives are busier than ever. Especially since impatience can mess things up forever.

Sometimes I wonder what would've happened if the Yankees had lost patience with me when I was a terrible catcher my first couple of years. What if Dickey hadn't been so patient in teaching me? Maybe I'd have had to go back to work in the shoe factory in St. Louis, I don't know.

When I was managing the Mets in 1973, we were in last place. The papers said I was getting fired. But there were still two months left in the season, we had to play the teams we had to play, so I said it's "not over till it's over," and it wasn't. We stayed patient, never panicked, got on a little roll, and made it to the World Series.

When I was a Yankee coach in the early 1980s, we had a skinny first baseman on our minor-league Nashville affiliate. Because he wasn't pulling the ball we were going to trade him. But I urged some of the higher-ups, don't touch him, give him time, he'll learn. So Don Mattingly stayed a Yankee. You could recognize the high potential in his talent. I told Mattingly I knew I was confident he'd succeed. When I became manager in '84, I put him in the lineup, and he won the batting title in his first full season.

Loyalty and patience were rewarded. It's different today. Sports is a lot of instant gratification, not patience. It has exploded into a huge business, actually a multibillion-dollar industry. Heck, Tiger Woods is probably worth a billion all by himself, and all power to him. He's that rare one person who can change a sport. In team sports, though, players get paid pretty darn well, too. I never begrudge anyone making millions, believe me. If the owners are dumb enough to pay it, I'd be dumb not to accept it, either. Of course, careers aren't long. The average major-league career is five years, even shorter in the NBA (four) and the NFL (three). What bugs me is when people assume that's why players are out for themselves—and point to a guy like Terrell Owens as an example. I'm not so sure he's typical. I'm just sure he gets too much attention.

I've always been a sports nut; I follow them all and still read the sports pages first. There's always some kind of drama or conflict. So-and-so isn't playing— and why not? Who's yapping too much? Whose job is in jeopardy? Not to sound like an old goat, but sometimes sports has gotten a bit sensationalized, too highlighted on the individual. Acrobatic dunks and monstrous home runs are hyped as plays of the day. I'm not a big fan of someone being his own biggest fan. If a Mickey Mantle or anybody back then ever stood and admired one of his homers, he'd be eating dust next time up. People stay connected to sports through fantasy leagues—they follow their handpicked players and their stats. That's nice, but what about attitude? Is he a good or bad guy in the clubhouse? Is he a whiner or a winner?

Seeing my grandkids play organized youth sports, I'm amazed what's happened. It's not kid's play anymore. It's more like professional leagues in miniature.

Everything's so structured, with all these travel teams, year-round practices, weight training sessions, recruiting, personal coaches—I mean, six-year-olds getting private baseball lessons? People come up to me and say, "My son's nine and has a good arm, what does he have to work on?" I look at them like they're nuts. I remind them the kid is nine years old. He needs to work on being ten. Jeesh, let him be a kid!

The one question I always ask parents: does your kid love it? That's important, because if he or she doesn't love it, they'll probably hate it.

I don't think kids have changed. Parents have. If nothing else, youth sports is a good social thing—or should be. You learn about being part of a team, camaraderie, playing by the rules, give-and-take with each other. If we had a disagreement, we settled it. When I was thirteen, me and my friend Charlie Riva got into a scuffle for a reason I can't remember. After we started hitting each other, I asked him, "What the hell are we fighting for?" And Charlie said, "I don't know," and we made up and resumed playing.

Playing sports as a kid in St. Louis was one of my happiest memories. We didn't have adults around us, we organized ourselves. What I learned most was cooperating with each other—teamwork—for the same goal. In our sandlot and YMCA league baseball games, me and Joe Garagiola played different positions because it was fun and it kept things fair. We all felt a responsibility to each other.

Do kids today have the same feeling? I don't know. I know they feel pressured by a lot of parents and coaches no matter what. At my grandson's baseball and basketball games, it's not terrible—I haven't seen any fights or anybody pay anybody to injure someone, like that crazy T-ball father in Pennsylvania. But it's not great, either. I just wish they'd let them just play, without yelling, "Choke up on the bat!" and "C'mon, get your head in the game!" Parents are so overinvolved. Everything's way too organized at way too young an age.

When kids are embarrassed and stressed, it's no fun. They get no fun competing or fun in working hard. They don't need so much pressure so young. Every kid on a team needs to learn about being part of a team— that means improving confidence and connecting with kids their own age.

One of my peeves is this premature specialization thing. To focus on one sport with year-round training isn't healthy, I don't think. It gets too intense, too many kids get injured, frustrated, burned out. I heard of a study saying you need about ten years and ten thousand hours of practice to become real strong at a sport. But when these parents hear this stuff, they try to do it all in a couple of years. They think it's the only way they can get that jump, get their kid a scholarship. Sometimes I think it breeds kids who aren't really having fun. They're not with their friends. They're more with professional coaches or instructors. If they get better skills, they don't get something just as important—appreciating being a part of a team, learning responsibility to others.

The only advice I ever gave my sons about playing sports was "Play 'em all," and they did. Not only did they become better athletes, they made different friends every season. That's what we did as kids—played every type of game there was. We played a lot of soccer in those days—way before soccer moms and SUVs—and always in winter. Soccer strengthened my legs; playing corkball and softball helped hand-eye coordination. We also played football and roller hockey in the street—whatever sport was in season.

Those were sandlot days, and I know they're not coming back. Back then there were gangs, not the vicious kind, just kids who hung out together. Ours was Stags AC—when we played ball, we had no uniforms, just T-shirts, and I guess we were like the Little Rascals (only there was no TV then, so we never watched the *Little Rascals*). We had no Little League, either. But we had it good—we had fun.

Now you wonder. Now there's hardly any neighborhood kids playing ball without adults. Now coaches and parents decide everything, and they go to extremes. Kids are so booked up—private instruction, travel teams, sports academies. When I hear about some eight-year-old getting a special coach for speed, power, and agility, I wonder, whatever happened to fun and games?

Back then, there wasn't a baseball team west of St. Louis. It was a simpler time. Basketball and football weren't popular—people lived baseball. It was the game America grew up on. For me and my closest pals like Garagiola, loyal sons of immigrants, it made you appreciate being part of a team. You needed all nine players to work together. Former New York governor Mario Cuomo, who also grew up playing the game in city sandlots, said, "I love the idea of the bunt, the sacrifice . . . that's

Jeremiah. The Bible tried to do that and didn't teach you. Baseball did."

Baseball taught us a lot. Now the game's bigger than ever; there's so much at stake because sports are such a dominant part of American life. Everything's so commercialized. But two things really haven't changed from the olden days when there was no team west of the Mississippi. First, the most successful teams don't have what's-in-it-for-me players and second, the most respected players are those who make their team better. The game of baseball is still the same, a team game. Sure, today's guys are wealthier and bigger and stronger, especially since they've all got these gymnasiums in the clubhouse. But the pressures to win are the same, then and now. Casey Stengel didn't have a hundred microphones and TV cameras in his face, like Joe Torre or Joe Girardi does now (not that Casey would have minded). But his biggest challenge was quite the same. "Finding good players is easy," Casey used to say, "getting them to play as a team is another story."

One spring training, asked who his regular third baseman would be, Casey said, "Well, the feller I got on there is hitting pretty good and I know he can make that throw, and if he don't make it, that other feller I got coming up has shown me a lot, and if he can't, I have my guy, and I know what he can do. On the other hand, the other guy's not around now. And, well, this guy may be able to do it against left-handers if my guy ain't strong enough. But I know one of my guys is going to do it."

Actually, we all knew who and what Casey meant. The first "feller" was Gil McDougald. "That other feller" was Andy Carey. "My guy" was Bobby Brown.

That's another thing. In those days, the Yankees didn't have names on the back of the uniform. Actually they've never had them . . . and probably never will. On the Yankees, the only name that's important is the team name on the front.

Businesses today want that same attitude. Job interviewers are always asking whether someone's a team player. What business doesn't want people willing to pitch in, help others, and work together? Who doesn't want efficiency and success? I think teamwork is an individual skill—the willingness to work hard, to set an example.

The greatest team guys are the ones with great work ethics. Playing with DiMaggio for five years, I learned he kept a book on every hitter and was always in the right place. I can't tell you how much our pitchers loved him, since he probably won more games with his glove, always being in the right position, than his bat.

When you're on a team or on the job, you spend an awful lot of time with your teammates or colleagues. In our day we had eighteen-hour train rides. We banded together, no jealous bone among us. We'd play cards, have a few drinks, go to movies—we were friends. Early on when we'd play in St. Louis, I'd have a bunch of guys come to my family's house for a little boccie and one of my mom's Italian feasts. Nobody called it a "team-building activity" or "building cross-functional relationships." It was just another shared experience. The more you share, the more you trust.

In major league baseball, the average career's only five years. So there's less sharing, less trusting, less commitment to the team. Every player always says he's there to help his team win, but you wonder. Is he playing for his contract or for his teammates?

Nowadays, more people look for jobs, not careers. More focused on their work, they don't communicate well or try to help others. That doesn't build a team. Perhaps that's why businesses look to sports for strategies of teamwork. Joe Torre and Mike Krzyzewski could quit their jobs tomorrow and spend the rest of their lives giving speeches on how to get individuals with different backgrounds and skills to mesh. Back in the 1960s, Vince Lombardi, the best football coach ever, said it good: "Individual commitment to a group effort—that is what makes a team work, a company work, a society work, a civilization work."

Nobody really called those Green Bay Packers or our Yankees teams "team players." But looking back, that's what we were. We won a lot and didn't want the winning to stop. Whatever was for the team good—sacrificing at the plate, changing positions, making each other laugh—we all did our part. There was always an expectation of success—didn't matter who you were or what your role was. Bobby Brown, who was my roommate in the minors, probably wanted to be a doctor as much as a ballplayer. He was our regular third baseman from 1949 to 1951, but he would pinch-hit and platoon much of his career. His was an unusual career—he attended Stanford, UCLA, and Tulane and missed a couple of years in the Korean War. Bobby was always busy with his medical studies, even when we roomed together in Newark. That's when one of those famous stories about me got out. One night after a long double-header, we both went back to our room. I was reading a comic book and Bobby some big medical book. When we turned off the lights, I told Bobby I enjoyed my story and asked him, "How'd yours come out?"

Everybody on the Yankees respected Bobby Brown, because he worked constantly. On the road, he'd call up the opposing team to see when he could get in the stadium to take early batting practice—and he'd hit for over an hour. Bobby retired when he was only twenty-nine. But as a teammate, you couldn't find any better. Being a Yankee meant a great deal to him, and he was one of the best clutch players we ever had. Bobby hit .439 in the World Series, almost half his eighteen hits going for extra bases.

Bobby was always there if you needed help. In my rookie year, I was nervous, real nervous on July 18, 1947, when friends from my neighborhood on the Hill organized a Yogi Berra Night for me in Sportsman's Park. I had to make a speech and was skittish. So I asked Bobby Brown for help. He just told me to keep it short and simple. He wrote it out, and I memorized the two sentences and practiced them on Bobby at least a dozen times. When I got to the mike in front of everybody, I said it just like Bobby wrote: "I'm a lucky guy and I'm happy to be with the Yankees." Then I guess my nerves took over, because the next line came out, "And I want to thank everyone for making this night necessary."

Playing with guys like Bobby Brown and winning all those championships with the Yankees, I realized it didn't take great players, but team-first players. Virtually all my teammates on those Yankees teams were great team guys, meaning we were as good as we had to be.

Let me end by saying sports and life are different today than in those days, but in a way they're really not. No, we didn't have $250 aluminum bats as kids. There was no round-the-clock sports on TV. There were no sports psychology and visualization and hypnosis. When people say there was more loyalty in our day, maybe there was. But I remind them that guys like Babe Ruth, Willie Mays, and Hank Aaron all got traded. And I remind them, too, that on a team, the most important thing isn't the accomplishments. It's the relationships. Being on a team isn't just being a member; it's giving of yourself for the team good. It's collaborating, sacrificing, trusting, and working together. Working together works.

Uniform Policy

Wearing a uniform . . .
promotes unity. Everyone's
equalized. That's sort of the
feeling you get wearing
the Yankee pinstripes. You're
part of a special collective.
The players come and go,
but the Yankee uniform
remains the same.

I ALWAYS THOUGHT THERE'S something proud about wearing a team's uniform, even better if it fits. It means you belong to something. It's like an honor. So you have a responsibility to those wearing the same uniform. Break a rule or do something foolhardy, you embarrass the uniform. You embarrass yourself and your team. Wearing a uniform—whether you're a cop or a coffee shop waitress—carries a responsibility and dependability. To those one serves and those wearing the same uniform. I think the reason schools promote wearing uniforms is because it promotes unity. Everyone's equalized. That's sort of the feeling you get wearing the Yankee pinstripes. You're part of a special collective. The players come and go, but the Yankee uniform remains the same. And as one of the team's announcers always says, no names are on the back. Of course, some people think the Yankee uniform can make you do things you normally don't do. Does it?

Well, it does something. It makes you realize you're part of an amazing tradition. When I played in the minors, we wore hand-me-down Yankee uniforms. I don't know whose old woolen jersey I wore, but Charlie Silvera was always thrilled that he wore Lou Gehrig's old pants when he was starting out in Class D ball.

Nowadays, nobody wears baggy flannels anymore; there's no more hand-me-downs. But anyone who puts on a Yankee uniform can't ignore the history of it all. It's not like another set of working clothes. When you see it, you know what you're seeing. It's the same pinstripes Ruth, Gehrig, Henrich, DiMaggio wore, all those guys. If every kind of uniform comes with responsibility, the Yankee uniform comes with an added kind. Don't think every guy in a Yankee uniform doesn't know it, either. Joe Torre played and managed a long time for the Braves and the Cardinals. He's been in baseball almost fifty years and always says the Yankee pinstripes still give him goose bumps. When players like Alex Rodriguez come here and put on the uniform for the first time, they tell you they feel something, too.

Carlton Fisk let it be known he always hated us, being a big part of the Red Sox–Yankee rivalry in the 1970s. But I always liked him. I'm partial to catchers, and Fisk was one heck of a good one. You had to like his work ethic and his being true to his sport. His rivalry with Thurman Munson only reflected his passion. You don't last twenty-four seasons without passion for the game. Near the end of his career, he was playing for the White Sox in Yankee Stadium, and Deion Sanders was just beginning his baseball life with the Yankees. Even then Sanders showed he was sort of a show-off

It never gets old putting on the uniform. At spring training each year I observe a lot by watching Jorge Posada, who should be a lifetime Yankee, too.

and self-absorbed. In one at-bat, he didn't bother to run out a pop-up. And that really bothered Fisk, who confronted him, real angry. He reminded Sanders that the pinstripes on his uniform stand for pride. Don't embarrass the guys who've worn them.

Uniforms are more than a fashion statement. They're a team's identity. It's like what Jerry Seinfeld said about fans: They don't really root for players, they root for a team's laundry. I still like that the Yankees still don't put players' names on their backs. The team's identity is more important.

Growing up, uniforms to me were sort of a big deal. Mainly since we never had them. It's so different now—a kid can't even play T-ball without a uniform. Back in my day, every kid in St. Louis neighborhoods belonged to a gang or a club. Our team, the Stags AC, joined an organized recreation league. All the teams were sponsored by local merchants who provided the kids with uniforms. All except us. I think the shopkeepers on the Hill didn't really appreciate baseball. So me and Joe Garagiola and the rest of the Stags had no uniforms—and hardly enough equipment. We spent a dollar to have T-shirts printed with "Stags" on them and probably looked like the Dead End Kids in our overalls and old pants. But I'll tell you, we got so motivated to beat the teams with uniforms. The next year, all the Stags were breaking up to go to other teams. Joe and I got asked to play for the Edmonds, which was sponsored by a restaurant. We were fifteen and proud as can be because we had our very first uniforms. I told Joe we finally looked like real players. When the Edmonds won the championship, the restaurant threw a big victory dinner for us.

Looking back, that was a good business lesson. Be true to your sponsor, they'll be good to you. I just hope uniforms don't get crazy like those race car drivers'. It's strange enough that teams are always changing shirts, wearing alternate uniforms all the time. Obviously it's all about merchandising. Teams even change their traditional colors, which I guess is a money thing, too. But the pinstripes just don't change. At least not in nearly a century. DiMaggio used to say his greatest thrill in baseball was pulling on a Yankee uniform every day.

Let me say this: if anyone thinks the Yankee uniform always makes guys improve or play bigger, it's not true. For some wearing pinstripes is like being in jail—not everyone can handle the New York atmosphere. Nothing's automatic. If you put a bunch of has-beens in pinstripes, they'll probably play like has-beens. But I think some guys do better as Yankees because of the other guys wearing Yankee uniforms. When I played, there was a togetherness and teamness on our teams, even with newcomers. Roger Maris wasn't too bad with Kansas City and Cleveland, but he was something else when he came here. Luis Arroyo was just a so-so pitcher until we got him in 1960; for two seasons he became our Mariano Rivera.

No uniform makes the person something he or she isn't. But wearing a uniform—firefighter or military or school—makes you part of a team. It should give a sense of belonging and pride. I'll always remember when I reported to the Newark Bears in 1946 and the trainer threw together some odd-shaped uniform for me. The pants were too big, the shirt too small. I accepted it, but when he gave me a frayed cap that barely resembled the Newark cap, that was too much. I was only twenty years old. But I felt if I was good enough to be on this team, I was good for a decent cap. So I ordered the guy to get me a better one. He saw I was angry. Then he pulled out a new one from the equipment bag. At least I looked like part of the team. To me that was important.

To this day, I'll almost always wear my Yankee cap. It's still my team.

You, a Manager?

When people ask me what really makes a good manager, I say two words: good players. . . . All that strategizing stuff is overrated. Games are won or lost by how well the players play, not how the manager manages.

WHEN PEOPLE ASK ME what really makes a good manager, I say two words: good players. More than anything, it's what makes a manager good, because without good players, your results won't be that good. In baseball, a manager can play percentages, play hunches, crunch numbers, and juggle lineups. He can be as good a strategist as a chess master and that's swell. Only he's not the one running, fielding, pitching, throwing, or hitting.

All that strategizing stuff is overrated. Games are won or lost by how well the players play, not how the manager manages.

Little League or peewee hockey or youth soccer is the same thing. The coaching part is getting them to learn and work together. It's not terribly different than managing a major-league ballclub. It's managing people. It's convincing each player that what's best for the team is not always best for him or her. It's being firm or unafraid of your judgment. It's figuring a way to get the best out of each person's ability.

The good ones leave a lasting impression. I never hear a Hall of Famer not mention his youth or high school coach during induction speeches. As I said, where would I be without a great coach like Bill Dickey? That's why I'll always be grateful for his patience and encouragement and learning me his experience.

Nowadays, businesses look to sports for how to motivate people, how to manage. Does it work? I don't know. I just know that plenty of managers and football or basketball coaches give expensive speeches and write books about the secrets of managing or leadership. Is getting the best out of a $10 million athlete the same as motivating a customer service rep? Who's to say? Sports teams are measured by wins and losses. Business teams are measured by something different, although a team effort is a team effort. A team is usually a good team when everyone knows their job and does it. If they don't, the manager or the coach is the one on the line.

Managing the Yankees is no walk in the park. There's pressure that will always be there. Joe Girardi probably feels like Miller Huggins felt eighty years ago. He knows he darn well better win. I've always said you could observe a lot by watching, and that's what I did as a player-coach in 1963, sort of my apprenticeship for managing. I replaced Ralph Houk, who was moving to the front office. When Ralph asked me if I wanted to manage, I said manage who? He said right here, the Yankees. Without really thinking, I said fine by me. As it turned out, Baltimore and Boston were also interested in me as a manager.

When I was asked to become manager of the Yankees back in 1964, I wasn't positive that I could do it. Lots of people weren't sure, either. When I came home after the big announcement, even my son Larry, who was thirteen, looked at me and said, "You, a manager?"

The Yankees offered me a two-year contract. But since I was still uncertain about the job, I asked for one year. I also got a $10,000 salary cut. Looking back, I was a real fool on that, so I don't dwell on that decision too much.

When I do look back, I learned that managing is no magic mystery. It's common sense. The main thing is to be yourself, not somebody you're not. Control what you can control, because you can't control everything; you can't control who you work for. When I was manager of the Yankees in 1985, I was fired after sixteen games. Working for George Steinbrenner in those days, stability was a fantasy. Someone called him a bouncer in a blazer. Whatever he was, he was a regular manager changer. Change to him always meant better. Billy Martin came and went five times. Bob Lemon was gone after fourteen games one year. Dick Howser was fired after winning 103 games. Only a few months before I got fired, Steinbrenner called me a fine, patient man. His way of saying I'd soon be an ex-manager.

Usually a team that starts off good builds belief in itself. It expects more of itself. But if you struggle early on, it's the manager who'd better keep the faith. And be calm and positive. Don't panic. Like I say, it's not over till it's over. To me patience means never giving up when you're down. We won the pennant in 1964 although it seemed gloomy, especially with injuries to our main guys. When we lost a bunch in a row in midseason, I could tell we were pressing. So I just reminded everyone the world wasn't coming to an end. Relax.

That was my approach to managing the Mets in 1973, and we were in last place in late July. There was talk everywhere that I might get fired. Nothing I could do about that except stay even-keeled. All along I knew we were due for a good streak. I reminded our guys it'll come and we'd be okay. Soon Tug McGraw started the chant, "You gotta believe," and we beat the teams we had to beat and made it to the World Series.

What did I learn? I learned what Chuck Tanner once said is true. Tanner managed my son Dale and those good Pittsburgh teams in the 1970s and always had a sunshine way even when things got gloomy. "There are three secrets to managing," he said. "The first secret is to have patience. The second is to be patient. And the third, most important secret is patience."

Even with the Yankees, patience and calm doesn't hurt. I was a coach on the 1978 team when Bob Lemon took over for Billy Martin. You'd look at Bob's face and never tell if we were winning or losing. He was unflappable, that's how he was as a great pitcher. When he took over in '78, we were fourteen and a half games behind the Red Sox. Bob used to say that if he were emotional, the players would have one eye on him and the other on the game. He never took credit for our comeback in '78, but everyone knew his quiet calm was a huge reason. His calm built confidence, especially for guys who needed it, like Reggie Jackson and Lou Piniella. You never saw nervousness in Lem's eyes. Never saw his head down if the team was down. He'd just

As a Mets coach with my son Dale in 1965. I never got real involved in my kids playing sports, except to encourage them to play them all and have fun.

reassure you with "Hey, Meat"—that's what he called everyone—but the players felt he knew them like a father knew his kids.

I'm not saying mellowness is a managing or coaching necessity. Some great ones are yellers. Some have chair-heaving tempers. Yet they're levelheaded when it counts. Piniella can scream like a banshee, that's him. His temperament, that's what helped make him such a good player. If he didn't get emotional over umpires or his team's bad play, he wouldn't be himself. He's calmed a bit over the years, but he's still got that volcano in him.

There's nothing wrong with being nervous, either. Every big game I ever played or managed, I'd get a few butterflies. Jim Leyland's a real good manager but looks nervous when he wakes up. They say he makes coffee look nervous. But his nervousness is also his intensity. Like Willie Mays used to say, "If you're not nervous, you probably don't care."

If you ask me, there's bad nervous and good nervous. Some of the best managers are stomach-churning wrecks. But if they're loyal, they care, and they're intensely focused, that's a good nervous and it rubs off on the players. Bobby Cox is normally low-key, a real good player developer and evaluator. Bobby knows the game—I coached with him on the Yankees in 1977. I knew he'd be a real good manager because he's patient and absorbs everything. He's also confident and enthusiastic about the game, although he's nervous every day, right from the first day of spring training.

Funny, Atlanta called me after the '77 season about the manager job. It didn't bother me that the team was bad, I just wasn't sure about moving south. The job went to Bobby, who was only thirty-six but knew what he was doing. He got the franchise turned around and did the same in Toronto with an expansion team. How'd he do it? He watched and learned a lot coming up through the Yankee system.

Bobby was an infielder on lousy Yankees teams in the late 1960s, but he watched how his manager, Ralph Houk, handled players. He asked lots of questions of the pitching coach, Jim Turner. As a coach, he saw how Billy Martin ran a game.

If you want to learn to coach, learn every day and learn from the best. Bobby's way of running the ballclub is his way. But he learned a lot when he was learning on the Yankees.

Bobby understands how hard it is to play on and manage bad teams. No matter what, he's never dogged a player in front of the team or the press. He always treats every guy respectfully, showing leadership in different ways. One way is being early. Bobby's always the earliest one at the ballpark, even when he was managing in the Yankees' low minor leagues. If you're managing a hardware store, you've got to be in the store. If you're managing a ballclub, you've got to be in the ballpark.

A manager is like a head of the family—leader, teacher, and disciplinarian. As a baseball manager, I always tried to show poise and patience and let players play through mistakes, because mistakes are learning tools. When a player's afraid to make them, he'll make them. If you learn from your mistakes, then success won't be a mistake.

Sure, patience has its limits, and patience isn't necessarily passiveness. Nowadays, even high school coaches feel immense pressure to win. It seems lots of college and professional coaches live on some kind of tightrope. Strain and fatigue come with the job. I never heard of an angioplasty until I heard coaches were getting them.

Managers know how to manage a game, but many can't manage stress. It's tough. A lot of real good ones—Earl Weaver was only fifty-two when he retired—quit before it became too much. (He used to call his top reliever, Don Stanhope, "Full Pack," because that's how many smokes he'd go through when Stanhope came in.)

As Leonard Koppett, a good guy and a great baseball writer, used to say, "What do managers really do? Worry. Constantly. For a living."

People think because my name is Yogi that I didn't worry because I was into yoga or meditated. Not quite. When I was about fifteen and playing American Legion ball, we didn't have any dugouts. So I'd fold my legs on the ground and sit with crossed arms. My friend Bobby Hofman said I *looked* like a yogi, and soon everyone started calling me Yogi. It's just how I sat.

Guys deal with stress differently. In the 1950s lots of us smoked cigarettes because nobody knew better. Once I was on a billboard in Times Square blowing smoke rings in a Camel ad. The company used to send cartons of cigarettes to my house every month; it was either nice of them or they were trying to kill me.

As a manager, I'd sneak a smoke once in a while. When things got worse, I smoked more. But I quit a long time ago and feel a lot better. Now I ease my mind by playing golf and working out on the treadmill.

It's nice to see coaches and managers who don't get so worked up or let daily stress get the best of them.

Managing the Yankees in 1984, with Stick Michael behind me. Stick was a great team man as a player, scout, coach, manager, and general manager and helped build the championship teams of the late 1990s.

Joe Torre has that inner calm. So does Terry Francona. They don't let much of anything affect them, or they don't show it. Truth is, most of their managing is really done in the clubhouse. They've built loyalty through relationships with their players. They boost confidence in a low-key way. They motivate through trust and respect—same as a guy like Tony Dungy, the Indianapolis Colts coach. Football's more emotional than baseball, but Dungy has a kind of emotional intelligence. He's got that calm and control that helps keep his team confident and productive.

The big challenges for any coach or manager are keeping your wits, not losing control, keeping your players motivated and confident. Whatever's broke, try to fix it, especially a player's confidence.

When I managed the Mets in 1973, McGraw was our best reliever and going through a horrendous stretch in midseason. Tug was usually a loosey-goosey fellow, a free spirit. But he was a frustrated mess, so much so that he even talked about quitting. Me and Rube Walker, our pitching coach, called him in, told him we needed him and would help him find his old self. We convinced him to become a starter again, at least for a few games. Tug was reluctant at first, thinking it would mess him up more.

As it turned out, Tug pitched more carefree as a starter. Mechanically he was the same. But mentally he got more relaxed. Then we moved him back to the bullpen, where he got confident again, and he was sensational in September. One of the biggest reasons we won the pennant that season.

Confidence isn't easy to get and it's hard to keep. Especially in a game like baseball. Failure is frequent.

But every bad or losing situation can be turned around. Any manager who sees a problem shouldn't ignore it. Talk about it or deal with it, or try to do something different about it, or it might get worse.

A big part of a manager's or coach's job is keeping players in a good frame of mind. Distractions are something that bothers you. It could be pain or fatigue. A family or off-field problem or a mass of media asking questions. Distractions are not part of the game, but they affect it.

Being in New York all these years, especially with a fishbowl team like the Yankees, there's always been more distractions and pressures because there's more of everything. The only way to focus 100 percent is not worrying about things you don't have to worry about. Playing in fourteen World Series, sometimes in front of seventy thousand fans and sometimes including the president, it was hard not to feel some jitters or awe. Everyone gets nerves. But after the first few pitches, I'd settle in and shake off the shakes.

Preparing for any big game, I'd prepare like it was any normal game. Never change my same routine. Sure, I'd be kidding myself to ignore a game's extra importance. But why dwell on its importance since it's already more important? Why get stressed? If a catcher goes out there a little nerve-racked, how can that be good for the pitcher's confidence?

Mental distractions happen. Worrying or over-thinking can creep into one's mind. That's why football coaches call time-outs to "ice" a kicker in pressure situations. Even pitchers try to freeze hitters. Sometimes they wait and try to get them to lose focus or rhythm. Hitters with those set routines—touch helmet, tap shoes, adjust batting glove, take practice swing, fix glove again, dig dirt in batter's box—are trying to get comfortable. So a pitcher has to unrelax him. He can shake off the catcher, he can take extra long, whatever he can to keep the hitter guessing or overthinking.

I'm no psychologist. But I know positive thinking can make you think good or concentrate better. If you're preoccupied with something, it can become a distraction. During the 1956 World Series, I was worried a lot about my mother back in St. Louis. Diabetes had gotten her bad, and she was scheduled to have surgery to remove her leg. I had trouble not thinking about her. Yet all Mom was worried about was *me* having a good World Series. After Larsen's perfect game, I called her up and she asked me to hit a home run for her the next day. Maybe she thought I was Babe Ruth. Whatever, I was trying like heck to do something, but didn't, and we lost 1–0 in ten innings. In game 7, I admit I wasn't thinking about any home run, only winning. As it happened, I hit two home runs off Don Newcombe that game, and we won the Series. I later told people those homers were for Mom, but I'm sure I hit them because I wasn't thinking about hitting them. The mind usually concentrates on one thing at a time. For two hours that day, all I thought about was doing my job, winning.

A good coach or manager helps get his players to think what they have to think about. He shows calm under pressure. If the pressure's on, he takes it off.

That's what Casey Stengel and Joe Torre did real well with the Yankees. They diverted the attention to themselves. Casey would talk double-talk for "my writers," the reporters who covered the Yankees. His stories rambled and took detours. But he understood what he was doing. He understood what the newspapermen needed. He also understood that to win, everybody was needed. Our Yankees teams never won the same way. Casey found the strengths and capabilities of his players and had a knack of putting them in the best position to succeed.

Casey and Joe couldn't be more different, but they were a lot alike. They did what they could to decrease the pressure. Especially for players who put extra pressure on themselves. Joe had a knack for getting guys caught up in the pressures of playing in New York to relax a bit. Casey would try to get through to Mickey Mantle, who always pressured himself too much. "One time I was especially gloomy over the way I was going," Mickey said once, "and Casey made me a speech about how baseball should be fun and that a man who doesn't get fun out of the game was not going to stay loose and do his best."

Joe has the same philosophy. And he's as good as they come with the media, who respect him because he respects them. He makes their job easier. And makes his players' jobs easier because he knows what it's like. Joe was one of the best hitters in the game, the National League's MVP in 1971, and played wherever his teams needed him—catcher, third base, first base. He knows the game's hard enough to play without full concentration. That's why he's such a good mental manager. If he benches a big-name player, he explains it to him. If the team is losing, Joe absorbs blame. If a controversy is brewing, Joe snuffs it. He's a manager anybody would want.

Casey Stengel knew he could always lean on me, calling me his assistant manager. Here he's congratulating me for making the Hall of Fame in 1972.

Joe's a good friend, one of the best people I know in baseball. I managed him with the Mets in 1975, near the end of his playing days, and playfully remind him that he's the reason I got fired. One game in July, Joe hit into four consecutive double plays, tying a record, and I was gone soon after. Joe says he wasn't to blame, it was Felix Millan's fault of always singling before he came to bat.

Joe happened to be one of the last player-managers in baseball. The Mets made him one in 1977, his first managing job. That dual job is impossible today. I learned it wasn't so easy years earlier. As I said, I was a player-coach for the Yankees in my last year (1963). The idea was to ease me into being a manager the next season. When I did become manager, I made Whitey Ford, who was still our best pitcher, also our pitching coach. We already had a great pitching coach in Johnny Sain, but he had a contract dispute with the front office after the '63 season.

So I asked Whitey to try it. He was the smartest pitcher I knew. It was kind of radical, being the only pitcher–pitching coach in the game. Yet it was working fine and Whitey himself was pitching great—until he got hurt. Then he got so worried about his bad hip and shoulder problem and whether he'd recover, it got hard for him to focus on the other pitchers.

By next year, I was gone. Whitey continued his career, but his pitching-coach duties were over.

Managing and coaching in sports have changed today. Now there's more responsibilities because everything's so specialized. In every sport there's more gizmos and statistics to help make decisions. There's so many specialty coaches, too. When I rejoined the Yankees in the mid-1970s, they hired a coach specifically to hit grounders and fly balls to Reggie Jackson. Now college and NFL teams have armies of assistant coaches, almost one for each position.

Overall, I see a lot of coaches, not a lot having important input. Why have coaches if you don't use them? As a manager, Torre always reminded me of Gil Hodges when I was coaching the Mets. He hung out with his coaches and valued their loyalty. As important, he valued their say.

In the 1950s managers like Leo Durocher and Charlie Grimm were also the third-base coaches. Then you only had maybe three- or four-man coaching staffs. Everybody did everything. Casey instructed our outfielders, and Bill Dickey, our first-base coach in the 1950s, became one of the early batting coaches. It was an extra assignment then, nothing like today. Now hitting coaches are like private tutors, and they become ex-hitting coaches when a team slumps. People say I was probably the first "bench coach" when the Yankees created a spot for me in 1976. My spot was sitting next to Billy Martin, and I'd give him my opinion when asked. Billy liked bouncing ideas off me. He knew I'd know what was going on and referred to me as his "morning newspaper."

Now everyone has a bench coach and a coach to monitor the bullpen. As well as nutrition and conditioning coaches and coaches who just watch video, and, of course, the first-base, third-base, and pitching coaches. Managers oversee them and twenty-five players every day. And managers have to manage the media, one of the toughest parts of the job. Still, I always wonder when a losing manager or coach says, "We didn't show up," or "We weren't ready to play," or "I didn't do a good job preparing my team." Mostly I wonder why. Wasn't the game on the schedule? What the heck was going on in the clubhouse that nobody was ready to play?

It's a given that everybody at some point is tired or physically beat up. Sure the season's a grind, especially in baseball, with coast-to-coast plane trips, day game followed by night game, day after day with few off-days. Back in my day we had eighteen-hour train rides and doubleheaders on most Sundays. Everyone gets a little tired when you're always weary. But you can't think about it, because the game is more mental than you think. If you're not sharp, you're not emotionally ready and are more apt to make mental mistakes.

Few things can deflate a team more than mental mistakes. Bonehead baserunning, an outfielder throwing to the wrong cutoff man, a fielder forgetting how many outs there are. It shows you're not ready to play, mentally. It happens, but it shouldn't.

When I was coaching for the Mets, Gil Hodges insisted that mental mistakes not happen. Gil was a good manager—low-key with a quietly strong presence. Once in a while but not often, he'd have a meeting to set things straight. One was before the 1969 season, when he reminded the team they'd lost thirty-six one-run games the year before. He said if we could cut out avoidable mistakes, we'd win a good many of those.

But in mid-May we'd just lost a couple of one-run games, partly because of mental boo-boos. One was one of our pitchers not getting off the mound to cover first.

Another time one of our guys was trying to stretch a double into a triple with two outs. Gil kept a lot inside; I'd say he kept his poise 99 percent of the time. But he wasn't one to forget or forgive players who brain-locked or didn't hustle. After the last loss, he shut the clubhouse door and blew his stack for a good ten minutes. He didn't mention anyone in particular, but everyone got his message. Losers make mental mistakes.

We went on to win a hundred games that season and, of course, the World Series. When people say the '69 Mets were a fluke or a miracle, I disagree. To me it was twenty-five guys who played the game right doing the right things. On the field, every player's mind became alert. Everyone put all out. When you get everyone thinking like that, it's a winning attitude; that's what Gil did with the Mets.

Managers shouldn't embarrass their players, especially not in front of their teammates. If you do, you could lose the guy's confidence or affect his attitude. I think players can play with fear. They can't play without enthusiasm. I think Clete Boyer, a good third baseman on our teams, lost his spirit a little when Casey would unintentionally embarrass him. Thing is, Casey wasn't always sold on Clete's hitting, and in the first game of the 1960 World Series he pinch-hit for Clete in the first inning. Sometimes you can't build back up what you tore down. Clete was just one of those guys who'd never be president of Casey's fan club.

Johnny Blanchard was another of those guys. He was our third-string catcher and never really got a lot of chances. One day Casey asked him if he felt he could hit and Johnny said he could. Then Casey asked if he felt he could catch and Johnny said sure. So Casey said okay, catch the next plane to Denver—that's how he told him he'd been sent to the minors.

Casey could be like that. He could be harsh. He was a lot like John McGraw, since he learned most of what he knew when McGraw was his manager in the 1920s. McGraw bruised a few feelings, too. With younger players, it's different. Sometimes you got to baby them, build them up, show them confidence.

That's what we did with Mel Stottlemyre in 1964. When Whitey Ford was out, we needed somebody to take his place in the World Series. So we had to put our trust in a twenty-two-year-old rookie with only a few weeks' experience in the majors. Mel always said he was awestruck being a teammate of Mickey and Whitey, but he didn't act it. He came from a little place in Missouri nobody heard of. How many towns have a population of ten? Anyway, I started him in big games down the stretch and he helped save us.

Reporters thought I was crazy pitching a rookie against Bob Gibson. But I think Mel was confident because we showed him confidence. All Whitey and I told him was: keep the ball down, we believe in you. That's it. He pitched beautifully in game 2, and I started him in game 5 and again in game 7 on two days' rest, all against Gibson.

Unfortunately, Mel didn't win the last one, and I got fired the next day. As it happened, the Yankees went downhill with some bleak years. But Mel won twenty games three times during that stretch.

He had a great mental attitude. And he became one heck of a pitching coach, with the Mets in the 1980s and the Yankees in the 1990s. That never surprised me. Mel always had a good listening ear, like any good coach. With all his pitchers, he was part psychologist, part mechanic, part supportive big brother.

As a young pitcher, Mel absorbed Whitey's calmness and advice and went on to calm and advise a lot of pitchers himself.

As a manager or a coach, you're dealing with adults, with professionals. You can't get overly emotional or browbeat them, or they would see right through you. Maybe it worked fifty or sixty years ago with hard-driving control-freak managers. Players were at their mercy. They listened up or were sent out.

Now it's different. You don't much see a manager or a coach publicly berate a player for mistakes. Only maybe if he's doing something embarrassing or avoidable. Like failure to hustle. Showing you don't hustle is like showing you don't care. You can't teach hustle or coach effort, but you can correct it when it doesn't happen.

Back to '69 with the Mets. We were playing Houston in a doubleheader and Gil called time out. Then he started a slow walk all the way out to left field. He was removing Cleon Jones, our best player, from the game. He did so because Cleon didn't hustle after a ball. There was talk that his leg was bothering him. That didn't matter. What mattered was Gil's message: if you don't give 100 percent, you're no good to the team.

Few good managers or coaches stand for lackadaisical play. If you stand it, you allow it. Whitey Herzog, for one, never tolerated nonchalance. I always remember Whitey as a good hustling player when he came up in the Yankee system in the 1950s. Because of Casey

Stengel, he learned what he knew about fundamentals and defense and hard-nosed hustle. Those were the trademarks of the championship teams he later managed in Kansas City and St. Louis.

Whitey's a good man, a heck of a baseball man. We were together with the Mets in the 1960s when he ran the farm system. To this day, he blames me for ending his career prematurely. When he was playing for Kansas City in 1959, he crashed against the low fence in right in Yankee Stadium to catch one of my drives. He hurt his back and never really was quite the same. I remind him it was his fault for robbing me of a homer.

Whitey insists the game's changed because players are more pampered. Maybe not softer, but richer. He believes these big contracts make players too statistics-driven. Not always interested in sacrificing for the team. Still, a manager has to do whatever to prevent lazy play and lack of effort, even and especially if it's his star player. You can't blame Willie Randolph for benching Jose Reyes over not running out a grounder. Or Bobby Cox for yanking Andruw Jones in the middle of an inning for not going all out after a fly ball.

Believe me, it's not just today. I was in the Yankee dugout thirty years ago when Billy Martin pulled Reggie Jackson for loafing in the outfield in Fenway Park. And I was there a half century ago when Casey Stengel pulled Mickey Mantle for not hustling down the first-base line.

Hustle, which really means to play 100 percent or more, also means pride. Without it, you'll lose. One thing fans won't tolerate is perceived lack of hustle. They perceive indifference. The only thing dumber than not hustling or making a dumb mistake is repeating it.

As a manager you expect all-out effort, you expect respect. Just after I took the Yankees job in 1964, I told a reporter from *Life* magazine, "Handling of pitching is 80 percent of managing. The rest is being a strong leader—keeping your men in line and in a good frame of mind. There are a couple of Yankees I'll have to keep my eyes on, but most of them are mature ballplayers. I believe they respect me. Respect, that's the big thing. Without it, a manager's dead."

I'll be honest. I always felt I had the players' respect, everyone played hard for me. Looking back, the famous harmonica incident on August 20, 1964, hurt and helped at the same time. We'd just lost to the White Sox, our fourth straight loss. Obviously I wasn't in the best mood. I didn't exactly get cheerier when Phil Linz started playing "Mary Had a Little Lamb" in the back of the team bus. When I yelled for him to knock it off, he didn't hear me and kept playing. So I went to his seat and knocked it away from him, which became a big flap. Frank Crosetti, one of our coaches who'd been with the Yankees for thirty-three years, called Linz's playing an act of defiance and one of the worst things he'd ever seen.

I fined Linz, we talked it over, and everything was smooth. Since I was usually so even-keeled, my outburst at Linz surprised people. Truth is, Linz was a valuable utility guy who stepped in and did a great job all year, always played aggressively. It was more me blowing off steam than insubordination. When I later joined the Mets as a coach, I recommended we get Phil in a trade and we did.

After the harmonica incident—even today Linz signs his name with a musical note—we played like I knew we could. Maybe the incident sparked us, I don't know, but I know we rallied to win the pennant. It would be the last Yankee pennant for twelve more years.

Honestly, I thought reaching game 7 of the World Series that season with an injury-marred team wasn't too bad. Thinking I'd be congratulated and awarded with a contract extension, I got fired the day after the Series. There were different reasons given, but I wasn't told any. Later, I learned the decision to fire me after the season had been made in August, which only proves what I've always said. In baseball, you don't know nothing. Even today, few managers or head coaches feel real sure about their security. Somebody has to get blamed if a team underperforms or doesn't win the championship. What rich-guy owner or demanding alumnus doesn't expect to win? Teams that don't win can't replace all the players. Plus it'd be admitting a lot of mistakes. It's simpler for a boss to admit one mistake and fire the manager. And that goes back long before George Steinbrenner.

But one thing that's never changed. Managers usually get too much credit when they win or too much flak when they lose. Casey Stengel had lousy teams in Brooklyn and Boston, never managing them past fifth place from 1934 to 1943. He didn't have the players or a future as their manager.

Managing the Yankees was another story. I remember when we came back from a 3–1 deficit in the 1958 World Series to beat the Milwaukee Braves. Casey stood up on a baggage trunk and proclaimed to the writers, "I couldn't have done it without the players." He was jesting, but he never minded getting credit.

Casey was like every manager in every game he managed. He was the decider. But he never decided the results. His players did.

If every team is like a family, the manager or coach is like the parent. He's responsible for the players. Sometimes he needs to discipline them. Sometimes he has to ego-soothe them. Sometimes he has to answer and alibi for them.

Don't get me wrong, being a manager is something I never regretted. It was baseball, and that's what I knew. It was fun managing and winning a pennant in both leagues. Getting fired three different times in five years wasn't so fun.

So here's what I learned through watching and observing managers and coaches for over sixty years. There's good ones and lousy ones, and the good ones can have a positive influence. A good one can make a difference with calm and patience and encouragement. A not-so-good one could be the reason the team under-achieves. But winning alone doesn't necessarily make someone a good coach or manager; losing doesn't always make someone a bad one, either.

How does one judge? People judge Gene Mauch as one of the best ever managers. I thought he was pretty good, too. I remember playing against him in an American Legion tournament game in Hastings, Nebraska, in 1942. He was a scrappy player and helped his California team beat our St. Louis team. And they said he couldn't win big games.

How good was he as a manager? In 1962, he was Manager of the Year, and his Phillies team finished in seventh place. Truth is, in all his twenty-six years managing in the majors, he never won a single pennant. Never got in the World Series.

Yet Mauch would regularly get the best out of his players. I was in my first year managing the Yankees in 1964 when his Phillies team blew the pennant in the last couple of weeks. To this day, he's second-guessed for pitching his two best pitchers on two days' rest. Sure it was a mistake. But ask any baseball man, Gene Mauch was shrewd, demanding, tough, an excellent teacher. He knew the game inside out, used his whole roster, and his players gave it their all and more, and that's a good way to judge a manager.

Again, Casey Stengel and Joe Torre didn't win many prizes with their previous teams. But they were already good baseball men. When they got to the Yankees, it didn't hurt when they got better players. They got better results. Like Casey used to say, the easiest way to win a ballgame is to make sure the players on your bus are better than the ones on the opponent's bus.

Nobody knew baseball better, nobody managed longer, than Connie Mack. He was like George Washington in the dugout, a great tactician, smart, patient, kindly, one of the early "player's managers." He won 3,731 games, the most in history. He also lost 3,948 games, but that's not why he's in the Hall of Fame.

My first manager, Bucky Harris, was another well-liked guy. When he was twenty-seven he was the "Boy Manager," and his Washington Senators beat out the Yankees in 1924 and 1925 for the pennant. He managed a real long time. Players were always loyal to him, and he stood by me as a struggling rookie in 1947. We won the World Series in his first year with the Yankees.

One heck of a manager, if you ask me. He won 2,157 games over his career. He also lost 2,218, and that's not why he's in the Hall of Fame, either.

When I first took over as manager of the Yankees in 1964, everyone wanted to know what kind of manager I'd be. Would I manage like Casey Stengel? Would I be like Ralph Houk? I told them I'll manage like Yogi Berra. What that was, I wasn't sure, but I wasn't going to be an entertainer or ruthless or fit someone else's idea of what type of manager I should be.

Being a baseball manager was no lifelong dream. My dream was always to play. Managers are like the establishment. They convince players to conform. I wasn't the big conformist, but as a kid, I liked organizing our pickup games and planning it all out. Our field was once an old clay mine by the city dump. We leveled the ground, and I convinced my buddies to dig a hole to put in the chassis of a junked car for the dugout. Later, I'd try to wake up the earliest to claim the field at Sublette Park or Macklind Field so we could play there all day. We had no football field on our block, so I painted ten-yard green stripes on my street. Joe Garagiola always said I was always managing no matter what game we played—baseball, football, soccer, roller hockey. Mostly I felt lucky to get to play. Some kids in our neighborhood couldn't be bothered playing ball and wound up bad. If it hadn't been for all those games, maybe I'd have been one of those Dead End Kids, who knows?

Looking back, I learned the enjoyment of playing ball and learned to get along with everyone I met. The further you get along in sports, the more you learn, but you learn that you never stop learning. And sometimes you learn that you never know.

Early in the 1955 season, which was the middle of my career, I did an interview with Edward R. Murrow on *Person to Person*. I was thirty and coming off my third MVP season. I didn't remember the interview, but someone recently showed me an old tape of it. When Murrow asked what I wanted to do after my career, I said hopefully stay in baseball, maybe as a coach. When he asked about managing, I emphatically ruled it out. Too many headaches, I said.

But near the end of my playing days, I didn't rule it out. Heck, I'd been playing the game, day in and day out, as a boy and a man. I knew the game, the importance of loyalty, of doing what's best for the team. Then the Yankees asked me.

Casey used to call me his assistant manager, because whenever he asked my opinion, I gave it. Especially when it came time to remove a pitcher. Casey was smart because he was smart enough to know he didn't know everything. But he also could see things in his players they didn't see themselves. Sure, Casey depended a lot on me. We'd have maybe sixteen doubleheaders a year, and he usually made me catch both games. "How ya feeling, young fella?" he'd ask me before a game. I'd tell him my back ached, my shoulder was stiff, my hands were bruised, and I was bone tired. "Good, you're batting fourth," he'd say.

Index

Page numbers in italics indicate photographs.